What Others Are S[aying About] *Sticky Lea[ders]*

Business Leaders

… illuminates the principles of innovation from an in-the-trenches perspective. If you're interested in harnessing the power of serial innovation, you should read this book.

—*Robert Alpert, Atlas Capital*

Osborne is a serial innovator. His ideas, concepts, and strategy are worth emulating by anyone who wants to successfully innovate, no matter what the field of endeavor.

—*Bill Boyajian, Bill Boyajian and Associates, Inc.*

Here's a fresh point of view from a real-life serial innovator on a subject everyone talks about but few get right.

—*Bob Buford, founding chairman, Leadership Network; author,* Halftime

Game-changing advice. Larry Osborne has been a guiding light during my own company's rise to success. I sincerely hope none of my competitors ever read this book.

—*Russ Carroll, CEO, Miva Merchant*

Very helpful ideas and experiences designed to assist successful entrepreneurs and innovators in both the for-profit and social enterprises.

—*Bill Cockrum, Price Center for Entrepreneurial Studies, UCLA Anderson Graduate School of Management*

Once again Larry Osborne has written a book filled with wisdom, practical application, and insights that will help you innovate and fulfill your God-sized dreams.

—*John Jackson, president, William Jessup University*

Filled with hard-to-learn lessons. Osborne has a unique combination of gifts: a keen sense for teaching the Bible as well as for leading in the corporate boardroom.

—*Gerry Krippner, president and CEO, Balda HK Plastics, Inc.*

Inspiration and practical advice from someone who has successfully leveraged innovation to grow his organization to the top of his field.

—*Kouji Nakata PhD, organizational development consultant*

This is an amazing book, just like all the rest of Larry's books. I always buy them in bulk. You should too.

—*Carolyn Osborne, Larry's mom*

A practical tool set for enabling innovation and overcoming stagnation. ... Keep this one close when you are moving through the change curve or when you hit the wall.

—*Dick Poladian, chief operating officer, Lowe Enterprises, Inc.*

You'll find Osborne's latest book to be comprehensive, focused, and immediately useful ...

—*Timothy Stripe, co-president, Grand Pacific Resorts*

I wish I'd read *Sticky Leaders* twenty years ago. It's a roadmap for understanding the counterintuitive patterns of innovation ...

—*Kevin Wilson, president and COO, Heska Corp.; founder, Cuattro Medical, Cuattro Software, Cuattro Veterinary*

... a breath of fresh air ... Osborne doesn't sweep under the rug the harsh realities of innovation and staying competitive in business today. His poignant perspective has helped me stay innovative in the high technology world of software.

—*Rick Wilson, president, Miva Merchant*

Nonprofit and Church Leaders

I'm always amazed by Larry's ability to bring deep understanding of proven solutions to the leadership challenges and issues that so many of us face.

—*Scott Chapman, The Chapel, Chicago*

Every book that Larry Osborne writes forces me to think in ways I had never thought of before. *Sticky Leaders* is no exception. It challenged me, chastised me, and cheered me on. It will do the same for you.

—*Wayne Cordeiro, New Hope Christian Fellowship*

I wish I had this book thirty years ago. It's full of wisdom. Practical. Relevant. It's a home run. I'm adding it to our leadership's required reading list.

—*Chris Dolson, senior pastor, Blackhawk Church*

Like the book of Proverbs, Larry is always filled with incredibly helpful and practical wisdom for leaders. This book is a must-read for those in leadership.

—*Mark Driscoll, founder, Mars Hill Church,*
Resurgence; co-founder of Acts 29

My expertise is in the nonprofit world. What I like about this latest book from Larry is its plainspoken truth about innovation and the development of the next generation of innovative leaders.

—*Dr. David Fletcher, founder, XP-Press, 5Macro*

Larry Osborne is an innovative leader who consistently sees the world from a different angle than the rest of us. If you're an innovator or think you want to be, read this book.

—*Dave Ferguson, lead pastor, Community Christian Church;*
NewThing Network

I've watched Larry Osborne innovate firsthand. He's a world-class innovation leader. Let him empower your dreams with this goldmine of a book.

—*Ron Forseth, vice president, Outreach, Inc.*

Larry is a contrarian. When everyone else nods their heads yes, he's often shaking his no. But there is no contemporary Christian leader who writes with more ingenuity, creativity, and insight about leadership. In many ways, he's a modern-day Solomon.

—*J. D. Greear, pastor, The Summit Church*

… graduate-level counsel on leadership. I wish I had read it forty years ago when I stepped into leadership. Great wisdom from a recognized innovative leader.

—*William J. Hamel, president, EFCA*

Osborne has an uncanny knack for finding patterns behind both success and failure, and he communicates them brilliantly in *Sticky Leaders*.

—*Noel Jesse Heikkinen, pastor, Riverview Church*

Osborne's breadth of experience with people and organizations makes his latest book essential reading for those who want to make a powerful impact.

—*John K. Jenkins, senior pastor, First Baptist of Glenarden, Maryland*

As always, Osborne delivers a fresh perspective that is persistently practical. If you think that innovation is mysteriously intuitive and can't be taught, this book may surprise you.

—*James Long, Managing Editor,* Outreach

Once again, Larry brings us sage wisdom in his highly practical and readable style ... a must-read book with insights you can't find anywhere else ...

—*Will Mancini, Auxano*

... honest and practical steps for planning, evaluating, and increasing innovation. Larry's insights will increase any leader's impact on their organization.

—*Mel Ming, founding partner, Leadership Development Resources*

Larry's uncommon sense and ability to see reality from 30,000 feet is what makes him the go-to advisor for leaders from all tribes. Read this book with a highlighter and pen. You'll overuse both.

—*Ryan Meeks, founding pastor, Eastlake Community Church*

Larry Osborne helps us take what Scripture says about leadership and apply it to our lives and the organizations we have been privileged to lead.

—*Perry Noble, pastor, New Springs Church*

Inspiring, equipping, and gut-wrenchingly practice. This book by Larry Osborne, a serial innovator, is a gift to entrepreneurial leaders.

—*Brian Orme, editor,* Outreach

In a culture obsessed with the new and the innovative, Larry Osborne deftly discloses the secret to true innovation ... If you aspire to be an innovative leader, you need this book.

—*Ed Stetzer, president, LifeWay Research*

In the thought-provoking contrarian style we've come to expect, Larry Osborne has produced another valuable resource for nonprofit, church, and business leaders alike.

—*Todd Wilson, Exponential*

Other Books by Larry Osborne

STICKY LEADERS

LARRY OSBORNE

ZONDERVAN®

ZONDERVAN

Sticky Leaders
Copyright © 2013, 2016 by Larry Osborne

Previously published as *Innovation's Dirty Little Secret*

This title is also available as a Zondervan ebook. Visit www.zondervan.com/ebooks.

Requests for information should be addressed to:
Zondervan, 3900 Sparks Dr. SE, Grand Rapids, Michigan 49546

This edition: ISBN 978-0-310-52948-4

The Library of Congress cataloged the original edition as follows:

Osborne, Larry W., 1952–
    Innovation's dirty little secret : why serial innovators succeed where others
fail / Larry Osborne.
        pages cm.– (Leadership network innovation series)
      ISBN 978-0-310-49450-8 (hardcover) 1. Creative ability in business. 2.
Leadership. I. Title.
    HD53.O83 2013
    658.4'063–dc23   2013017692

Cover design: Brand Navigation
Interior design: Matthew Van Zomeren and Ben Fetterley

Printed in the United States of America

HB 02.08.2019

To Nancy, Nathan, Rachel, and Josh,
who have brought immeasurable joy
and meaning to my life

To Wally Norling,
who believed in the dreams of a young man
and taught me to believe in the dreams of others

CONTENTS

Part 7
LEAVING A LEADERSHIP LEGACY

Part One

START WITH AN EXIT STRATEGY

PREPARE FOR FAILURE

The One Thing Leadership
Gurus Will Never Tell You

T his started out as a book about innovation. But it ended up being a book about change and innovation. That's because change and innovation are twins separated at birth.

Change alters what we've always done. Innovation produces something that has never been done. But both have one thing in common: the more that they're needed, the more likely they are to be fiercely resisted.

That's why two of the most challenging tasks of leadership are successfully navigating the change process and introducing innovation. It's why I wrote this book. In the following pages we'll explore what it takes to introduce lasting change and innovation. I'll expose the dirty little secret that no one wants to talk about, and we'll examine the counterintuitive practices that successful change agents and serial innovators use to greatly increase their odds of their success.

Let's start with a look at the dirty little secret that those who extol the benefits of constant change and radical innovation never want to talk about. It's most often swept under the rug or ignored in the hope that it will just go away. Yet its shadow looms over every attempt to break out of the box and try something new.

Make no mistake. It can't be avoided. It's the dark side of the creative process. If you have dreams of blazing new trails of innovation or championing major change, it will smack you upside the head before you're done.

So what is this dirty little secret that haunts our best efforts at bringing change and innovation?

It's simply this: most innovations fail.

They always have. And they always will.

It doesn't matter whether we're talking about a new product, a new program, or a new process. It can be a new company or even a new church. When it comes time to start something new or make a major change, the surest horse you can bet on is the one called Failure.

You'd never know this if you listen to the people who write and speak about leadership and innovation. They often make it sound as if out-of-the-box thinking, burn-the-boats risk-taking, and gutsy leadership are all it takes to win the race and rise to the top.

But despite the great press and sizzle that surrounds the idea of innovation and change, the fact is that most attempts at innovation and major change crash and burn. Even organizations and leaders who are famous for cutting-edge, innovative strategies have a far longer list of failures than successes.

Now I'm not saying that all of our great ideas are doomed to failure. I'm not saying that change and innovation are too dangerous to try at home. And I'm certainly not suggesting that change and innovation are unimportant or unnecessary.

No, the pundits are right. If we fail to innovate and change, we eventually will lose the race. We'll fall to the bottom of the pile and slide into organizational irrelevance.

But that doesn't change the truth that innovation always carries significant risks. Failure is far more common than most aspiring leaders realize and far more likely than the zealous advocates of innovation are willing to admit.

In fact, failure is an integral part of the change process.

AUTOS, AIRPLANES, AND THE INTERNET

Imagine for a moment that you had tons of money to invest when the combustible engine was first invented. Now imagine that you also had the foresight to grasp how profoundly it would alter the way we live, spawning new industries and radically changing our global culture, creating new pockets of enormous wealth.

Since you couldn't know which specific businesses would rise to the top, you probably would have "wisely" invested as broadly as possible in as many of the new automotive companies as you could find.

But if you had done this, you would have gone flat broke. Rather quickly, because almost all of the innovative startups in the automobile industry went belly up.[1]

The same is true of the airline industry. While manned flight has profoundly changed the way we live, if you had invested money in all of the early airline companies, you'd have nothing to show for it today. Most of them went under. Very few made any significant profits.

Ditto for the internet. It's an understatement to say that the internet has changed everything. But those who jumped in too quickly and invested in everything that looked remotely promising lost everything.

Why?

As always happens, innovation's dirty little secret showed up to crash the party. Despite its game-changing potential and all the talk about a new economy with a new set of rules, the old rules prevailed. And most of the bleeding-edge early adopters and the first-to-market companies (the darlings of the investment community) crashed and burned.

WHY CHANGE AND INNOVATION GET SUCH GOOD PRESS

So if failure is such an integral part of change and innovation, why even bother with it at all? Why does something so wrought with pain and disappointment get such good press?

One reason is the influence of a niche industry that has become big business. Billions are spent each year on seminars, training events, and books that promise success to leaders (and pretty much anyone else) who are willing to take a big risk to try something radically new.[2]

If you want to fill a room, sell lots of books, and charge up the troops, it's counterproductive to point to a high failure rate. In fact, it's a guaranteed way to cut down on sales and limit speaking engagements. So no one talks about it. Instead, the motivational gurus focus on stories of against-all-odds success and ignore the many casualties along the way.

A second reason why change and innovation get such good press is that most failures aren't all that spectacular or important. We never hear about them because they aren't newsworthy. A huge percentage of new initiatives never even get off the ground, and among the few that do, many crash and burn with little fanfare.[3]

Why?

Because if these failures aren't connected with our company or our employer (or something that makes the national news), we aren't likely to notice them.

The same holds true for new businesses, church plants, and other startups. There are countless failures. Think of the trendy new clothing store in the local mall. It used to be a Chinese takeout. Before that, it was a boutique wine shop. Each of these changes represents a failed dream, a likely bankruptcy, and a ton of heartache and soul searching. But if it wasn't our dream, our bankruptcy, or our heartache, we aren't likely to have noticed.

A third reason why change and innovation get such good press is simply human nature. We don't like to think about negative things, even if they're inevitable. How many people do you know who adequately plan and prepare for their death? The odds that we will die are astronomical. But most of us would rather not think about this inevitability—at least not right now.

It's the same with failed changes and innovations. They surround us. But we'd rather not think about them. We chalk up the failures of others to foolish ideas, bad planning, or inept leadership. We think we are different. We can't imagine the possibility that the changes we champion and the great ideas we have just might not be so great after all. We're sure that our ideas will succeed where others have failed.

This helps to explain why the dirty little secret of failure remains such a well-kept secret. Motivational gurus don't want us to think about it. And even though failure is incredibly common, most of these failures don't hit close enough to home to notice. On top of that, we'd rather not think about it — or plan for it. It's not as exciting and sexy as dreaming and thinking about our latest idea for the next big thing.

Yet that raises an important question, the question that drives this book: how is it that some people and organizations seem to defy the odds?

How is that some folks successfully innovate and change time after time? How do they overcome their failures? How do they maximize their successes? What is it that sets them apart? What do they know — and what do they do — that others don't?

Chapter 2

UNCONSCIOUS COMPETENTS

Why You Shouldn't Trust Everything Innovators Tell You about Innovation

Some innovators are one-hit wonders. They're like a band with a catchy tune that goes viral. They score a huge success and then are never heard from again.

Consider the infamous "pet rock." In 1975, Gary Dahl and his friends sat in a bar grumbling about their high-maintenance pets. Out of their grumbling, Dahl came up with the idea for a new pet — a pet rock. It would never need to be groomed, fed, or cared for. It would never get sick, disobey, or die. When Gary took his idea to market, it proved to be incredibly popular, selling more than 1.5 million units. Unfortunately, that was the last great idea he had. After the success of the pet rock, Gary's ideas weren't so successful.[4]

Sometimes an innovation succeeds because it's so novel and off the wall that it gains instant notoriety. But the problems with this kind of innovation are that it's hard to repeat, it doesn't take long for the novelty to wear off, and it's usually easy to duplicate. So it seldom translates to long-term success.

I once read about an innovative high school basketball coach who came up with the ultimate end-of-the-game play. Trailing by one point, with only a couple of seconds left on the clock, his team had the ball out of bounds. With one player stationed near the basket, he had the others run to the free throw line and suddenly drop to their knees and begin barking like dogs at the top of their lungs. As the other team turned to stare in disbelief, the ball was passed to the one player left standing under the basket. He caught it and easily made the game-winning shot.

Now that may be a great example of thinking outside the box (and barely within the rules). But I guarantee you, no matter how innovative and successful the coach's ploy might have been the first time, it had little chance of succeeding the next time the two teams met.

Some innovators and innovations are like that. They perfectly fit the time, place, and situation. They're incredibly successful. But it's a one-time deal. It can't be pulled off a second time.

SERIAL INNOVATORS

There is another kind of innovator and change agent at the opposite end of the spectrum. These folks aren't one-hit wonders. Instead, they pull off multiple innovations and major changes seemingly without a hitch. They are what I call "serial innovators."

When you see them from a distance, they appear to defy the odds. They seem to be immune to failure. But that's just not true. The truth is that they are just like the rest of us. They head down plenty of dead ends. They have lots of failures.

But they also have a special genius that keeps their failures from becoming fatal. And it's not what most people think. Their success is not found in their ability to avoid failure. It's found in their ability to minimize the impact of failure.

They have learned to fail forward—or at least sideways. They seldom fail backward. And even when they do, they know how to navigate the choppy waters of a failed change or innovation in a way that preserves the long-term credibility of their organization and leadership.

We'll see how they do that in a later chapter. But first, let's take a look at why it's incredibly difficult for most of us to learn much from these successful leaders. Contrary to what we might expect, many of them are clueless as to how they pull it off.

If you ask them for guidance, many of them will give you terrible advice. They will tell you to do all the wrong things. It's not that they are trying to mislead. It's not that they are frauds. The problem is that they are "unconscious competents." They do all the right things. But they have no awareness of how or why they do them.

UNCONSCIOUS COMPETENTS

When you ask an unconscious competent for the secret to his success, he'll tell you what he *thinks* he does, not what he actually does. It's similar to what a natural athlete does when he picks up a ball and instinctively makes the right move or throws the right pass.

Unconscious competents see and do things at a subconscious level far better than most of us could do with months of practice and preparation. They also usually have no idea that much of what they see and do is foreign and unnatural to everyone else. Which explains why they make great teammates, but lousy coaches.

I remember as a young man reading an article by one of the greatest baseball players of all time. He claimed that hitting the ball was relatively simple. All you had to do was watch for the spin of the seams to determine what kind of pitch it was, and then you just hit the ball based on the spin.

So I went out and tried his advice. It didn't work. I had no idea how the seams were spinning. I couldn't even see the seams. In fact, I could hardly see the ball. It was coming at me way too fast.

Not long afterward, I heard another former player being interviewed on the radio. He said he couldn't pick up the spin of the seams either. When he tried, the ball ended up in the catcher's mitt. Yet he was still able to hit a baseball well enough to have a lengthy career in the major leagues.

The truth is that despite what one of the greatest hitters of all time may have thought, his ability to hit a baseball involved far more than simply picking up the spin of the ball and hitting it. It also demanded incredibly quick hands, great balance, proper weight transfer, arm extension, an accurate knowledge of the strike zone, and a host of other things I could never get the hang of. But all of these things came so naturally to him that he hardly noticed them. Instead, he credited his success to something that actually had very little to do with his success.

Many of the most innovative and creative leaders do the same thing. Because they are unconsciously competent, they spout clichés about believing in themselves, taking huge risks, and making wild leaps of faith.

All the while, the real key to their success is not found in any of these things. It's not found in taking massive risks. It's not found in radical leaps of faith. What enables them to succeed is their instinctive and unconscious ability to know which risks are worth taking and what to do when things don't go as planned. But if you ask them to describe how they do it, they credit their success to something altogether different.

It dawned on me years later that the superstar who claimed that hitting a baseball was a relatively easy task still failed to get a hit more than 65 percent of the time. To this day, that statistic gives me a warped sense of encouragement. It reminds me that hitting a baseball — like successful change and innovation — isn't nearly as easy as some of the experts make it out to be.

CONSCIOUS COMPETENTS

Fortunately, there is another class of serial innovator. These are the innovators who are successful at innovating time after time and also know why and how they are successful. They are what I call "conscious competents."

Unlike unconscious competents, these innovators are self-aware. They know what they are doing and why they are doing it. And unlike the theorists and researchers who study and write about innovation, but have never pulled it off themselves, they know firsthand the nuances of innovating and leading change in the real world.

Ironically, conscious competents, while they are successful, are seldom "Hall of Fame successful." More often than not, they have more in common with a professional golfer's swing coach than the top money winner on the PGA tour. A good swing coach is almost always an excellent golfer in his own right. But unlike the superstar on the tour, the swing coach had to work a little harder at mastering the fundamentals in order to make the cut.

Frankly, that's my own story. Though I've had a great deal of success in my chosen field, these successes came neither quickly nor easily. In fact, during my first three years at the church I pastor, attendance increased by a total of one person. For those of you who are mathematically challenged, that's one-third of a person per year. Inspiring indeed.

During that time, just about every innovation and change I instituted failed. Along the way, I paid more than my share of "dumb taxes." But I also learned not to make the same mistake twice. And I carefully watched and learned as others made their own mistakes. I learned the fundamentals.

Eventually, the church took off. From a small group meeting in a high school cafeteria, we grew into one of the largest churches in America, gaining a reputation for innovation, organizational health, and national influence.

Then a strange thing happened. A steady stream of leaders (in both church and business settings) began seeking my advice. Seeing our growth and the success we had handling the difficult transitions that came with it, they asked for help navigating the choppy waters of their own transitions, looking for counsel as they sought to innovate and make major organizational changes of their own.

Frankly, it took me by surprise. I have theology degrees, not an MBA.

But I quickly learned that when it comes to growth, change, and innovation, there's not much difference between a church, a community organization, and a car dealership. The landmines, roadblocks, and paths to success are remarkably similar. When it comes to change and innovation, failure is still the norm. And the path through it is still the same.

In fact, some would argue that it's even more difficult to make major changes in a church or nonprofit environment because of the voluntary nature of the organization and relationships. Pastors and nonprofit leaders lack executive power. They have few, if any, economic levers to motivate people. If people don't agree with what they say or dislike the changes taking place, it's easy for them to bolt. It's a lot easier to find a new church than to find a new job.[5]

• ◉ •

In the following pages, we'll unpack the basic and transferable principles of innovation and change from an in-the-trenches perspective. We'll look at what it takes personally and organizationally to create an environment that fosters innovation and change rather than shutting it down. I'll be sharing examples from the church, the nonprofit world, and business, because those are the worlds I know best.

If you're a novice leader or a board member, my goal is to help you better understand and navigate the predictable risks and dangers of implementing new ideas and major organizational change.

If you're an experienced leader, my goal is to help you better assess the odds of success and failure *before* launching out, and to help you develop a workable (and sellable) game plan that will minimize the natural resistance to any new change or innovation.

And if you're a grizzled veteran, I hope to add some new tools to your belt. But I also expect that I'll be affirming some of the counterintuitive thoughts and insights that you've long had but have been hesitant to say out loud.

If you've long felt that the Innovation Emperor is naked, that the hype and promises are overblown, I'm here to tell you that you're not the crazy one. When it comes to innovation and leading change, it's the conventional wisdom that's crazy.

But I realize that it's not eay to be the only one shouting, "The emporer is butt naked!" Especially when everyone else is praising his wardrobe.

IT'S ALL BETWEEN THE EARS

How to Recognize a Serial Innovator

I t's not difficult to recognize a seasoned serial innovator or change agent. Just look for a track record of successful changes and innovations.

But what if someone is a fledgling innovator, just getting started? How can you identify those on your team who have the potential to become serial innovators but haven't yet had the opportunity to amass an impressive portfolio? And how can you make sure that they are freed up to do what they do best, creating the future, without blindly authorizing them to chase after every harebrained idea they can think of?

Frankly, that's not so easy to do.

First of all, most leadership teams and boards have a negative initial reaction to change and innovation. They're typically so busy dealing with the concerns of the present that they don't have the time or energy to think deeply about the future. The vision and passion of an innovator often come off as distractions rather than as windows to the future.

People who are knee deep in a sea of alligators don't have much interest in hearing someone's creative plan to drain the swamp someday. They just want another shotgun, and they want it right now.

That is why it's hard for most innovative ideas to get a fair hearing. Unless the innovator is also the primary leader (or someone near the top of the organizational food chain), most leadership teams and boards won't take the time to listen. This explains why most innovators have to leave and start their own organizations in order to try out their ideas. They have no other option.

Second, most leaders and boards have a strong bias to protect the past. That's not all bad. Someone needs to protect the gains of yesterday or they'll be lost.

But healthy organizations—those that remain healthy for the long haul—can't just focus on protecting the past. They must also think about creating the future, because if they don't, someone else will. And when that happens, all the gains they've worked so hard to protect will be lost.

Consider IBM. As a company, they held the future in their hands. They had the key patents, technology, manufacturing know-how, and sales force to bring the personal computer to market. But their top leadership decided to hamstring the development and sales of personal computers so they could protect the high-margin profits of their existing mainframe business. They essentially gave away the right to produce an operating system, preferring to focus on what was working for them at the time. All of this worked out rather nicely for Bill Gates and Microsoft, if not so well for IBM.

Or consider an example from the world of churches. Some churches insist on maintaining the same programing, ambiance, and worship style that helped them grow thirty years ago. While this protects the past and keeps their aging members happy, it also guarantees that their nursery will remain empty. And it explains why so many of them end up as feeder churches to newer churches with ministries that match today's date on the calendar.

The only way a leader and a leadership team can overcome this natural tendency to protect the past at the cost of the future is to find ways to identify and release the gifted innovators in their midst.

But how do you do that?

It starts with identifying them. And to do that, it's helpful to understand how genuine innovators (as opposed to mere dreamers and idealists) think and see the world. Three telltale traits set them apart from others. If you hang around them long enough, you'll see these traits cropping up in the words they use, the decisions they make, and the ideas they beg you to let them try. Here are the three traits to look for:[6]

1. A special kind of *insight*
2. A unique form of *courage*
3. Extraordinary *flexibility*

Let's take a brief look at each one.

A SPECIAL KIND OF INSIGHT

Genuine serial innovators and change agents have a special kind of insight. They have an uncanny knack for predicting what will and won't work and how large groups of people will respond to a new idea. At times it seems as if they can see around corners.

But it's not magic or clairvoyance. It's simply the way their brain works. They have a God-given ability to mentally model various outcomes, and to do so with blinding speed and uncommon accuracy.

They are a lot like a master chess player who sees several moves ahead (and the potential results of each move). Serial innovators size up a situation and quickly extrapolate what will happen if and when various options are taken. They not only see the natural consequences; they also see the *unintended* consequences that most people miss.

Yet if you ask them how they know these things, they'll often tell you that they "just know."

In reality, they don't "just know." They're actually processing a great deal of data at lightning speed. But since they do it subconsciously, they seldom have a clue what's going on between their ears.

If asked to defend their position or explain why they did something, they can usually give very good reasons. They make it sound as if they came to their conclusions in a highly linear fashion. But that's not what actually happened. When they explain their thought processes, they are usually reverse engineering something that came to them in a flash of insight.

A UNIQUE FORM OF COURAGE

Successful serial innovators and change agents also exhibit a unique form of courage. But it's not the wild risk-taking kind of courage that you might expect. They're *serial* innovators because they *don't* take crazy and wild risks.

Instead, they take carefully calculated risks.

Their courage is simply a matter of trusting their mental model. While everyone else is clamoring for more proof, they already have enough proof. They know there will never be enough evidence to prove beyond the shadow of a doubt that something that hasn't been done before will work. After all, it hasn't been done before.

But based upon the clarity of their mental model, they step out and take a risk that is in reality no more courageous than stepping out on new ice after you've watched a couple of trucks drive across it.

It may look like they take giant leaps of faith, but they don't. They don't hope their new ideas will work. They know they will work, because they've already seen the end game played out in their mind's eye.

In fact, I've found that most serial innovators and successful change agents are actually risk-adverse. They don't value risk for risk's sake. They know the reward is not in the size of the risk. It's in the quality of the risk. Like a card counter in Vegas, they're willing to place a big bet. But only when they know they'll win.

EXTRAORDINARY FLEXIBILITY

The third telltale trait of a successful serial innovator and change agent is extraordinary flexibility. I don't mean yoga-like flexibility. I'm referring to the ability to quickly change course. When things don't turn out as expected, they can turn on a dime. They're masters of the midcourse correction.

No one gets it all right all of the time. Life is too complex for that kind of perfection. But the same ability to accurately model outcomes on the front end also enables serial innovators to mentally model changing outcomes midstream, and to readjust in light of the new data.

Serial innovators are the ultimate realists. Contrary to what many people think, great innovators are not marked by a stubborn, hell-bent, I'll-let-nothing-stop-me devotion to their dreams and vision. They're marked by a stubborn devotion to the truth, even when it's not what they want to hear.

The idealist and dreamer will stubbornly go down with the ship. The serial innovator and successful change agent is not so stubborn. When the waves get too high, he grabs the rudder and changes course. Or as Jeff Bezos, the founder of Amazon.com, has pointed out, people who are right a lot of the time are the same people who change their minds a lot of the time, especially when the facts prove them wrong.[7]

HOW DID THEY GET THIS WAY?

I once believed that almost anyone can learn to mentally model outcomes in much the same way that most people can eventually learn to see the picture behind the picture in a Magic Eye drawing (even if it takes awhile). I assumed that all it takes is a teachable spirit, a willingness to work at it, proper training, and exposure to the right experiences.

I was wrong.

I now realize that serial innovators are born, not made. Just as someone with perfect pitch hears what others can't hear, innovators see what others can't see. It's in their DNA. They can't help it. They're weird.

RELEASING YOUR INNOVATORS

This doesn't mean that if you weren't born with these traits that you're shut out from innovative and creative leadership. Far from it. But it does mean that if you are going to foster a spirit of innovation and an openness to change within your organization, you will have to find ways to identify the fledgling innovators and change agents in your midst and then find ways to support some of their seemingly crazy ideas.

And that can be scary for a leader.

It's one thing to throw stuff against the wall to see what sticks when you're in startup mode. But it's another thing when you have a past to protect and existing congregants or customers you can't afford to ignore or drive away. Or to put it another way, it's easy to bet the farm when you have no farm to lose. It's not so easy when you have an actual farm with lots of mouths to feed.

I'm convinced this is why so many mature congregations, non-profits, and businesses opt to leave the cutting edge of innovation to startups and entrepreneurs.

It seems safer.

In the short run, it usually is.

But in the long run, it's a death wish. There is no long term safety in the status quo.

So how can we know when it's time to let our innovators make a major change or innovate and when it's time to hunker down and protect the gains of the past?

To be honest, there's no way to know for sure. Only time will tell if we've made the right choice. After all, no one can predict the future. Which is why the key to making the right decision doesn't lie in soothsaying or risk assessment. It lies in something most leaders never think about, something that serial innovators never leave home without.

It lies in a viable exit strategy.

Chapter 4

EXIT STRATEGIES

Why Your Exit Strategy Is Just as Important as Your Game Plan

Individuals and organizations with a positive track record of change and serial innovation of change and not only think and see the world differently. They approach the process of introducing change and innovation differently. They understand that brilliant ideas aren't always so brilliant once they're released into the wild. So along with their game plan, they have something most leaders don't think about. They have an exit strategy. They keep an ejection button close at hand, and they're not afraid to use it. They know that a viable exit strategy is just as important as (and sometimes more important than) a good implementation strategy.

A GRACEFUL WAY OUT

An exit strategy is simply a planned, graceful way out.

Think of it as keeping your options open. It can include everything from an escape clause to simply making sure that there's enough wiggle room for some serious midcourse corrections if things don't go as planned.

For example, consider the way a seasoned developer purchases real estate. Knowing that the pathway from a grand dream to a grand opening is full of potholes, experienced developers will "option" a piece of property rather than buying it outright. They pay a fee to keep it off the market while they confirm that they can get the funding and approvals necessary to complete the project.

To an outsider, these option payments may look like a waste of money. But if things go south, it provides a quick way out. After all, it's much better to lose some money on option payments than to own a useless piece of property you'll never be able to build on.

When North Coast Church needed to acquire forty acres in Southern California for a main campus, we paid nearly thirty thousand dollars a month in nonrefundable option payments to keep the property off the market while pursuing full entitlement.

Some folks thought we were nuts, especially since the approval process looked like a slam dunk. The land was already zoned for commercial use, and our project had strong support from the planning department and city council. With everything apparently lined up for success, why not just save the money and close escrow?

Here's why.

At the eleventh hour, a small group of neighbors filed a NIMBY (Not in My Backyard) lawsuit. No one saw it coming. They had lain low and waited until the last moment they could file suit. With only five minutes left on the clock, they turned in their legal papers.

They were also skilled and tenacious opponents. They delayed the project a couple of years. They forced us to jump through legal hoops that cost money and time. For a while, it was dicey. We weren't sure whether we'd get our approvals.

We eventually won the right to build our campus. But in the meantime, our leadership team's credibility (and my sleep) greatly benefited from the fact that we had an exit plan in place should the city or the courts decide against us. While it would have been horrible to lose all the money we'd spent on option payments, it was nothing compared with the cost of owning a multimillion-dollar, forty-acre white elephant. Had we lost, it would have been money well wasted.

Now compare that with the experience of another church I know. When a large parcel next to their campus became available at a fire-sale price, they were convinced that the timing and price was a God thing. They hurriedly put the property under contract, sold the vision of expanded parking and new buildings to the congregation, and bought the land.

Unfortunately, after acquiring it, they learned that the city leaders didn't share their enthusiasm. Instead of approving their project, the town council laid down a boatload of onerous requirements and costly upgrades as a condition of approval.

Today, that land still stands empty. The church can't afford the required upgrades to build on it, and they can't sell it for anywhere near the price they paid for it. Prospective buyers have deeply discounted the value knowing that they'll have to spend a ton of additional money before they are allowed to build.

But the greatest loss here wasn't to the church's bank account. It was the loss of trust and credibility the leadership team suffered. Though the bank account eventually was replenished, the pastor and his board have very little congregational trust to this day.

NEVER MAKE A CHANGE WHEN YOU CAN CONDUCT AN EXPERIMENT

There are several ways to keep your options open. Sometimes you may have to buy an escape clause. But more often than not, all it takes is carefully chosen words, using the right language and terminology to describe your vision. Whenever possible, describe any change or new initiative you propose using the language of experimentation. In other words, never make a change when you can conduct an experiment or a trial run.

Experiments provide you with lots of wiggle room. People expect that experiments and trial runs will need midcourse corrections. No one is shocked if they fail. And when they fail, the cost in lost trust and credibility is essentially zero.

Contrast that with what happens when a new initiative or major change is oversold or overhyped. The harder you push and sell, the more position papers you write and distribute, the less wiggle room you'll have.

Unfortunately, this is a hard concept for many leaders and organizations to grasp.

For most of us, once we've decided to move forward with a major change or initiative, we immediately move into sales mode. We use the language of persuasion. We try to convince the unconvinced, treating naysayers as obstacles to be overcome, and we become obsessed with proving we're right.

As a result, we tend to see any hint of compromise or retreat as a sign of weakness rather than as a sign of wisdom. And when this happens, we've effectively backed ourselves into a corner. There's no way out.

The language of experimentation provides exactly what unproven and untested ideas need most: plenty of room for midcourse correction—and sometimes, an escape hatch for bailing out altogether.

REDUCING RESISTANCE

I've already said this, but it bears repeating: people and organizations have a natural, knee-jerk resistance to anything that is new or different. Leading people through innovation and change is hard enough without galvanizing this natural resistance. But that is exactly what happens when a new idea or program is oversold.

The language of experimentation disarms much of that resistance. Here's why.

Most people (even late adopters and Luddites) will interpret the language of experimentation as a request to try something. They will always be far quicker to grant permission to try something than approval to change something.

I've found that many people who would fiercely object to anything that smells like change will passively step aside and let me try an experiment or engage in a trial run. Admittedly, they fully expect to see my attempts fail. But I don't care. All I need is the chance to see if it works.

The language of experimentation turns these potential opponents and saboteurs into bemused bystanders. If I'm right, I end up a hero. If not, I'm just a researcher who tried one more experiment that didn't work.

However, there is a time when it's best to move full speed ahead, to abandon your exit strategies and forgo this approach. It's when you're out of options and about to go under.

THE HAIL MARY PASS

Sometimes a desperate and dying organization needs to make the leadership equivalent of a Hail Mary pass. A Hail Mary is what happens in the final seconds of a football game when the losing quarterback fades back and heaves the ball down the field in the hope that something good (and lucky) will happen.

It seldom works.

But it sure beats giving up.

If your church, community organization, or company is about to go under, I'd encourage you to heave the ball down the field. Make whatever big and bold changes need to be made. You might as well do it right now, before the clock runs out.

Who knows, it might save the day.

Odds are it won't. But it might.

But remember this. Outside of a desperate situation in which failure is imminent, a Hail Mary pass is just a wasted play. For most leaders, the clock *isn't* running out. We have plenty of time. It's our patience that's running out. And a lack of patience is no excuse to neglect crafting our language so that it provides us with the wiggle room we need.

Hail Mary passes seldom work. But long passes, set up within the framework of the game plan, not only work; they often produce touchdowns.

EIGHT EXIT STRATEGY QUESTIONS

To help you and your team carefully think through the key elements of a viable exit strategy, I've put together a list of eight questions. You can use these questions to develop an appropriate exit plan before launching any new project, initiative, innovation, or major change in your organization.

But I want to be absolutely clear. I've never met a leader, a leadership team, or a governing board that uses exactly these same questions. In fact, I don't slavishly use them either. If you ask me at a conference or seminar to recite them, I won't be able to do so without a cheat sheet. But that's not because the questions are bogus. It's because they're the result of reverse engineering.

I've taken the thought processes and benchmarks that serial innovators typically use and reframed them into these eight questions. They represent an amalgamation of the most important factors serial innovators use to decide when it's time to move forward, put on the brakes, hit the gas, or bail out in order to live and try again another day.

You can apply these eight questions to any new endeavor or major organizational change you propose. If you take the time to work through them, you should have a basic, viable exit strategy in hand (just in case your latest great idea doesn't turn out to be so great).

Here they are.

1. How will we communicate this internally and externally in a way that provides maximum flexibility for significant midcourse corrections?
2. What will we do if everything goes more slowly than expected?
3. What benchmarks will cause us to keep going even though things are going more slowly than expected?
4. What benchmarks will cause us to pull the plug?
5. How will we communicate if we need to shut down the whole thing?
6. How will we communicate if we need to go back to the old way?
7. How can we limit and absorb the financial burden if this doesn't work?
8. What can we do right now to minimize the impact should this fail?

Part Two

IGNITING INNOVATION

Chapter 5

BEYOND AVANT-GARDE

If It Doesn't Make a Difference, It's Not an Innovation

Ultimately, it's not just the quality of an idea or the persistence of the leader that determines whether an idea succeeds or fails. It's also the environment.

Corporate culture (the values, traditions, and policies that guide a particular organization's behavior) is often far more important to the success or failure of a new idea than the brilliance of the idea or the doggedness of its backers. There are environments and corporate cultures that ignite innovation. There are others that foster, incubate, or accelerate it. And there are some that will kill it before it ever gets off the ground.

Before we explore the differences between these various environments (and what we can do to ensure that our own organizations remain innovation friendly), I want to clarify what I mean by the term innovation.

Long ago, I learned that people who use the same words don't always use the same dictionary. So here's my working definition, the one I've been using and will continue to use throughout this book. An idea, to qualify as a genuine innovation or successful change, must (1) work in the real world, and (2) be widely adopted within a particular organization or industry.

Both are equally important.

43

COUNTERFEITS AND SUBSTITUTES

Just because something is new doesn't mean it is an innovation or helpful change. The better mousetrap that nobody buys may be a clever and fascinating *invention*. But it's not what I call an innovation.

Consider the Segway. It was unveiled with great fanfare, and many marveled at how easy it is to balance, control, and move around. Many claimed that it would forever change the way people live and traverse in our major metropolitan cities. Now I would agree that the Segway is an incredible invention, ingenious in its design and engineering. But it hardly qualifies as an innovation or significant game changer—unless you're a mall cop.

The same is true for new and creative approaches to ministry. Many start with a bang and die with a whimper. A new approach can get lots of great press. It's assumed to be the next big thing. But if it fizzles out and doesn't last for the long haul, it's not an innovation or successful change. It's a failed experiment.

That's not to denigrate the value of failed experiments. I'm simply pointing out that trying lots of stuff that doesn't work isn't the same thing as innovating.

Admittedly, discovering what *doesn't* work is an important step toward real innovation. Consider Thomas Edison. He spent two years trying out materials that didn't work in order to discover a dependable and affordable filament for his incandescent lightbulb. But notice that Edison didn't rush to market every time he had a filament that appeared to work. Instead, he continued to experiment, leaving himself plenty of room for failure in case he was wrong, as he often was. Eventually, he hit the jackpot.

This distinction between experimenting and rushing to market is important because when we confuse innovation with great ideas, ingenuity, novelty, and change, we tend to implement every new thing we're excited about or think will work well on the false assumption that we're being innovative.

But rushing to market with lots of stuff that fails isn't innovative or creative leadership. It's lazy leadership. It won't make you a cutting-edge leader. It will make you a failed leader.

The same goes for the silly idea that we should change things for the sake of change. Making lots of changes won't make our church, nonprofit, or business more innovative. It will make it sick, giving it a bad case of organizational whiplash, which is not something to be proud of as a leader.

The secret to becoming a creative and innovative organization is not found in having lots of ideas, trying lots of things, or making lots of changes. It's found in having the *right* kinds of ideas, trying the right kinds of things, and launching the right kinds of products, programs, and initiatives.

BETTER IS NOT ALWAYS BETTER

Consider the QWERTY keyboard. It's the keyboard that most of us type on today. It was designed in the 1870s as a way to prevent the arms of a mechanical typewriter from jamming. It separated commonly used letters so that a fast typist wouldn't have to continually stop and unjam the keys. The result was faster typing on a mechanical keyboard. It was quickly and widely adopted.

But it has some problems. The way the letters are laid out, the left hand does most of the typing, even though it's the weaker hand for most people. The middle or so-called home row is used only about 30 percent of the time, even though it's the fastest and easiest row to use. Plus, the last time I looked, few of us type fast enough to jam the mechanical arms of a typewriter. Most people can't even remember what a typewriter looks like.

Faster, more efficient keyboard layouts have been invented. The best known is the DVORAK keyboard. It has been demonstrated that it is easier to learn and faster to type with. Yet it (like all the other attempts to create a faster and better keyboard) has failed to gain traction. It has never been widely adopted, despite its superior performance.

Many have studied and written essays explaining the reasons why. The DVORAK keyboard has become a celebrated case study for exploring cultural and organizational resistance to change. For our purposes, all that matters is that the "better" solution wasn't widely adopted or successful in the marketplace. It was an invention, not an innovation.

Faster, cheaper, and more efficient doesn't guarantee success.

Imagine, for a moment, that you were once president of a manufacturing company. After you rigorously tested the DVORAK keyboard, you found it to be much faster and better than the QWERTY keyboard, so you decided to buy the patent and flood the market. You built millions. If you did so, the company would still have warehouses full of unsold inventory. You and everyone involved with your scheme would probably be unemployed. Because when it comes to innovation, better is not always better.

Which, by the way, is one more reason why an exit strategy is as important as a launch strategy.

THE DIFFERENCE BETWEEN AN ARTIST AND A LEADER

Another important distinction needs to be made. It's the difference between *artistic* innovation and *organizational* innovation. This is a difference that is all too often ignored. I'm constantly amazed by the number of leaders (and pundits) who lump these two together when they advocate for more innovation. The unfortunate byproduct is confusion: it encourages leaders and organizations to take risks and behave in ways that are perfectly appropriate for artists, but foolhardy for leaders of organizations.

Artistic creativity is rooted in self-expression. It ignores boundaries, and it seeks to be unique and different. Anything that is fresh, anything that pushes the envelope, is highly valued.

It doesn't matter if the average person likes it, understands it, or puts it to use. In fact, if an artist becomes too popular or ends up being widely accepted by the masses, he'll likely be written off as someone who has gone commercial. He'll no longer qualify as a "real artist."

But organizational creativity is different. Leaders don't win awards for self-expression, for breaking the rules or being unique. They win awards for solving problems. And if the masses reject their solution, it's not a badge of honor. It's a sign of failure.

Whereas artists seek to express their creativity outside the boundaries, leaders and organizations express their creativity *within* the boundaries.

Think of the famous story of the *Apollo 13*. While the three astronauts on board were running out of oxygen, the ground crew was trying to build a makeshift oxygen filter using only the items that the astronauts had aboard their stricken craft. They didn't get to pick the materials, the colors, the timeframe, or the product. They weren't allowed to bend the rules.

To an artist, such constraints are unacceptable. They're devaluing and degrading. Even a commissioned artist hates to be given too many guidelines.

But within an organization, constraints are par for the course. Innovative leaders don't bemoan limits. They embrace them. The limits define the challenge. They are half the fun.

This distinction between artistic and organizational creativity is important because when leaders think and act like artists, they put themselves and their organizations at great risk. A leader can't ignore the rules. He can't be true only to himself, or paint whatever he feels like on the canvas of his organization. To do so is not gutsy and bold. It's irresponsible and selfish.

This is true even for an entrepreneur operating in startup mode. He has a lot more freedom to do what he wants than the leader of a mature organization. He can pursue his dream and do things his own way. But he still has to come up with a plan that is financially sustainable. There are still rules that define the path to success, and he must operate within those rules.

A starving artist is an iconic figure. But a starving entrepreneur is not.

I'll be the first to admit that there are some great stories about people who succeeded using an artistic approach to organizational leadership. They quixotically chased their dreams, risked it all, breaking every rule along the way. They bet the farm, burned the boats, and against all odds hit it out of the park.

We've all heard their stories. Motivational speakers love to tell them as a way to encourage us to take greater risks. But if we look closely at the truth behind the story, for every person who hits it out of the park that way, there are thousands more who swing for the fences and strike out, bankrupting themselves, their families, and their organizations.

Make no mistake, those who confuse the values and methods of artistic leadership with the values and methods of organizational leadership are the ones most likely to end up living like an artist—in need of a day job to survive.

• ◉ •

Successful innovation and change isn't found in the avant-garde. It's not an endless quest to be more creative, novel, and inventive. It's not even found in the search for the better solution. It's found in the *right* solution, the one that works and is widely adopted because people believe it makes their lives better.

And this points us to an important leadership lesson: When it comes to deciding what makes people's lives better, what makes the organization run more effectively, what's innovative rather than just creative and different, we don't get to make the call. The people do.

Chapter 6

INNOVATION'S MOST POWERFUL IGNITERS

Why Your Biggest Problems May Be Your Greatest Blessings

I'm not much of a handyman. Sure, I can fix stuff. That's not the issue. The problem is that when I get into fix-it mode, I start to fix stuff that's not really broken. I'll find something that's slightly off kilter, working at less than optimum capacity, or something that doesn't match up to my sense of aesthetics, and I'll start tampering with it.

Sometimes it works out well. I'll call my wife over to admire my handiwork, and she'll agree that it looks or works a lot better than before.

But most of the time, my attempts are just a waste of time. When I call my wife over to admire what I've done, she'll tell me that she can't tell any difference, and she will remind me that it wasn't broken to begin with. Far worse are the times when my tinkering with something that isn't working perfectly results in something that no longer works at all.

I hate trying to explain how I broke something by trying to fix it, especially when no one else thought it was broken.

Yet I know I'm not alone. Many of you have done the same thing. It's something that lots of leaders do. They tinker with anything that strikes them as less than ideal or fails to match up to their standards. They think it's the pathway to constant improvement and innovation. But most of the time they're just breaking stuff, and they end up destroying morale.

Serial innovators and successful change agents don't fall into the tinkering trap. They don't try to fix everything that's broken or improve things that aren't running perfectly. Instead, they focus on fixing the things that will make the biggest difference. They know that a better mousetrap, a more efficient keyboard, or an ingenious new mode of transportation won't change anything if no one wants it or cares.

So how do we identify the changes — the fixes — that will make the biggest difference? How can we learn what people care about, what they see as broken, and what they'll buy into if we fix it?

There are no easy answers. This is often more of an art than a science. But if you want to find the kinds of ideas that lead to genuine innovation, changed paradigms, and things that people actually want and use, start by asking yourself two simple questions:

1. What frustrates me most?
2. What's broken most?

It's in the answers to these two questions that innovation is most likely to be birthed.

Let me explain.

WHAT FRUSTRATES YOU MOST?

The first question you want to ask yourself is, "What frustrates me most?" Why? Because organizational innovation is often ignited by our deepest personal frustrations.

I'm not talking about low-level annoyances. I'm talking about gnawing frustration, the kind that arises when we're forced, on a recurring basis, to deal with something that makes no sense. It might be a bureaucratic process, an outdated program that wastes badly needed funds and emotional energy, or a maddening piece of machinery that never works right.

Most people, when faced with these kinds of frustrations gripe about it, mock it with sarcastic humor, or inwardly seethe. But beyond that, they do nothing to change it.

Innovators and successful change agents are different. They will gripe, whine, and tell sarcastic stories like the rest of us. But they'll also grab a sheet of paper and start imagining something different or head to the garage and start fiddling with that annoying piece of machinery. They can't help themselves. They're born to fix what doesn't work and change what they don't like. It's how God made them.

Here's the good news. You don't have to be a naturally born innovator to ignite the innovation process. You just have to be frustrated enough to believe there's a better way. You don't have to be the one who comes up with the better way.

Think of it this way. The innovators in your organization are like the running backs on a football team. They can't succeed alone. They need an offensive line to open holes for them to run through. Even the greatest running backs can't succeed without an offensive line, but an average running back can look like an all-star behind the bruising blocks of a great offensive line.

So if you're a leader who isn't particularly innovative, look for the people within your organization who are. Find those who share your frustrations but also have a list of things they'd like to try to make it better. Then take on the role of an offensive lineman. Use your position, power, and influence to open up holes for them to run through. Search for opportunities to give their new ideas a trial run. Let them experiment whenever possible. Become their benefactor and protector.

Most of their ideas will fail. But don't worry about that.

Just as in football, it takes lots of plays that go nowhere to get a few plays that score touchdowns. As a leader, your role is to make sure your innovators don't fumble and lose the ball on the plays that go nowhere. To do this, position their ideas as trial runs and experiments. And don't forget. Always make sure you have an exit strategy in place before you let anyone run with the ball.

WHAT'S BROKEN MOST?

The second powerful question you can ask is, "What's broken most?"

The organizations with a history of serial innovation are also the organizations with a long list of problems to be solved. Not much innovation takes place when everything runs smoothly or the future seems certain. It's the panicked and paranoid (or those backed into a corner) who innovate.

Problems are never fun, especially big ones. Most of us spend our lives trying to avoid them. But if you're a leader, they can't be avoided. So don't run from them. Don't ignore them. Embrace them and attack them. Your greatest insurmountable problems often will contain the seeds of your most significant innovations.

That's regularly been the case at North Coast.

Years ago we had a sanctuary that seated barely five hundred people, yet we had more than three thousand showing up each weekend. This would have been lots of fun if we were playing a massive game of musical chairs. But we were trying to do church.

Now, that might not sound like a problem. It might even sound like a blessing to some. But it wasn't. It was a mess. We were in danger of becoming like the restaurant that's always so crowded that nobody goes there anymore (no one except the foodies who don't mind the long wait and large groups of people celebrating special occasions).

For a church trying to reach people who don't go to church, this was a potential death knell. People who love going to church might put up with crammed facilities, bad parking, and weird time slots, but people who don't normally go to church won't put up with any of these things.

Putting up a "No More Room in the Inn" sign was also not an option. We didn't think the innkeeper was the hero of the Christmas story.

We had to do something. So we came up with a concept we called "video venues." The idea was to add simultaneous worship services, each one having its own live worship experience, style, and ambiance, but sharing the same sermon on a large video screen. We figured we could expand faster and cheaper by finding more rooms for video venues than we could by attempting to build a bigger sanctuary to accommodate everyone.

Lots of people thought we were crazy. Shoot, most of my staff thought I was crazy. "Who wants to watch a sermon on a big screen?" they asked. To most of them, it sounded like a glorified overflow room. And we all know what an overflow room is: it's a punishment for being late. Who would choose that?

Turns out, lots of people.

The first weekend, we offered Starbucks coffee and some danishes as a reward for those who attended. One hundred seventy-three people showed up. We filled a small room to capacity, twice. Within a couple of years, we had twenty-three hundred adults attending one of these venues each weekend. And though our church had grown to well over five thousand in weekend attendance, we had room for more.

Why did this work? It worked because while most things don't translate well on a screen (thus the dreaded overflow experience), teaching does. In fact, speaking works exceptionally well on a screen. It's easier for people to see facial expressions and other nonverbals. That's why in large rooms with the speaker on a screen, everyone beyond the seventh row watches the screen instead of the stage. They can see the speaker better.

Our biggest problem turned out not to be such a big problem after all. It led to an innovation that changed everything, in a good way. Since that time, we've built a beautiful new campus that can accommodate thousands more. But our new facility doesn't have a single, massive sanctuary. It has numerous large meeting rooms that house more than twenty worship venues each weekend. And we've added off-site video campuses as well.

As I write this, our weekend attendance is well over eleven thousand and continues to increase. Seventy-five percent of our congregation chooses to attend one of our video venues or a video campus, and we have the ability to scale this up to accommodate thousands more.

What was once a weird idea in a Southern California church has now become mainstream for larger churches across the country and around the world. Currently, more than five thousand churches in America use some sort of multisite strategy, with more churches being added every week. And it all started because we had an insurmountable problem, one we were unwilling to live with.

The thing that was most broken ended up igniting the innovation that now works best—our video venues and multisite campuses.

RIPE FOR CHANGE

It doesn't matter whether you are leading a church, a nonprofit, or a business. To identify the programs, processes, and policies that are most ripe for innovation and change, step back and ask yourself, "What frustrates me most?" And then ask, "What's broken most?"

When you've come up with your answers, attack the problem. Relentlessly pursue every possible alternative. You might not be able to come up with a solution on your own. But eventually, someone will. And I guarantee you, it won't be someone who accepts the status quo or who says, "That's just the way it is; there's nothing we can do about it." It will be someone who is frustrated.

To help you think through your areas of greatest frustration and the problems that are most ripe for change and innovation, here's a list of questions that you and your team can work through to prime the pump. These questions will help pinpoint the programs, processes, and mechanisms that are most ready for something different.

1. What is it that drives me crazy?
2. What are we doing that makes absolutely no sense?
3. What processes and programs seem to take lots of work, but bear no fruit?
4. What traditions are we putting up with simply because it has always been done this way?
5. What is the one problem that if we could solve it, most of our other problems would go away?
6. What's broken that seems to be unfixable?
7. What problems are we living with because everyone says, "That's just the way it is"?

Part Three

ACCELERATING INNOVATION

Chapter 7

WHY MISSION STATEMENTS MATTER

How Clarity Accelerates Innovation

Almost every organization has a mission statement of some sort. Sadly, many of these statements have little to do with what is actually measured, rewarded, or valued. They don't describe reality. They spout clichés and marketing slogans.

That's a shame, because an honest, clear, and concise mission statement can be one of innovation's most potent accelerators. But the kind of mission statement that keeps an organization focused and accelerates innovation doesn't just happen. It takes careful thought and honest reflection. It's more than plastering a cool slogan on a website or passing out new business cards.

To make a difference, a mission statement must have three essential traits. It must be ruthlessly honest, widely known, and broadly accepted. Each of these traits is absolutely critical. If your mission statement is missing any one of them, you'll have a three-legged stool with only two legs. No one can sit on it without falling over.

So let's take a careful look at each of these characteristics to learn why they're so important to innovation, and what we can do to ensure they're incorporated into our mission statements.

RUTHLESSLY HONEST

First, to be useful, a mission statement must be ruthlessly honest. It should reflect your organization's passionate pursuit, not merely your wishful thinking, your marketing slogans, or a spirit of political correctness. Anything less is disingenuous. And worthless.

It doesn't take long for people inside and outside an organization to recognize what the real priorities are. If your mission statement says one thing, but all of your decisions and actions pursue something else, the predictable result will be cynicism and confusion.

For instance, when a church claims to be "Proclaiming the Gospel to Everyone, Everywhere," but all of its programs serve its members and every tough decision errs on the side of keeping them comfortable and happy, you know that's not an honest mission statement. It's a wishful-thinking statement.

When a business claims to be "Providing World Class Service to All of Our Valued Customers," but acts like the DMV, that's not a mission statement. It's an indictment.

The same is true for the university that claims to be "Educating the Minds and Shaping the Character of Tomorrow's Leaders," but all of its polices are designed to protect the interests of tenured faculty and wealthy donors. It doesn't have an honest mission statement. It has an empty slogan.

It's what we actually do that matters. At the end of the day, organizations are just like people. They aren't what they want to be; they're what they *are*—the sum of the priorities they live by and the choices they make.

Yet despite the fact that no one wants to produce cynicism and confusion, it's no secret that many (if not most) mission statements fall short of being ruthlessly honest.

Why is that?

There are two primary culprits.

Confusing Mission with Marketing

Many leadership teams confuse mission with marketing. They fail to understand the difference between the two. Their mission statements sound like they come out of the marketing department.

WHY MISSION STATEMENTS MATTER

A mission statement should be aimed at insiders. Its purpose is to tell those on the inside of the organization where the bull's-eye lies. It's fine for outsiders to hear the statement and know it. It's fair for them to use it as a benchmark, to measure how well the organization is doing. But ultimately, the purpose of a mission statement is to tell everyone on the *inside* what we're aiming at. It's supposed to let them know what's most important.

Marketing is different. It's aimed at outsiders. Its purpose is to convince them to check us out, buy what we sell, or trust us more than our competitors.

When a mission statement morphs into a marketing slogan, it loses power. It becomes a declaration of what we want others to think about us rather than a forceful and honest articulation of what we're passionate about. It obscures the bull's-eye, rather than highlighting it.

Vision by Committee

Another enemy of the honest mission statement is "vision by committee." The more people you involve in the process of creating your mission statement, the more likely it is that you'll end up with a convoluted list of politically correct priorities designed to assuage the sensibilities of everyone involved. It will lack the precision of laserlike vision and the clarity that you need to define your mission.

This is a far bigger problem in the nonprofit world than in the business world. That's because churches, community organizations, colleges, and other nonprofits often function like quasi democracies.

I know of a church whose mission statement includes nearly everything a church could possibly do. It speaks of evangelism, discipleship, world missions, compassion, community impact, education, contextualizing the gospel, and a bunch of other stuff I can't remember. It's so long the pastor and the church leaders can't remember it either.

No wonder the church has long floundered. When everything is important, nothing is important.

And I know exactly how this happened. I don't have to ask.

At some point, the church formed a task force or a committee to come up with a revamped mission statement. Anything someone thought was remotely important was included (as well as anything someone thought someone else might think was important). No one had the guts (or authority) to speak up and say, "Hey, that might be a good thing, but it's not what we're really passionate about." Political correctness and the desire to honor everyone present wouldn't allow any cuts to be made.

I understand. I certainly wouldn't want to be the guy to speak up and label myself as being against the priorities on their long list. My bet is you wouldn't want to be that guy either.

Which is why vision by committee never works. Instead of producing an honest statement of passion and priorities, it inevitably results in a sanitized and inclusive statement that is more concerned with maintaining harmony than describing reality.

The vision by committee process may cause more of your people to feel involved. It may sidestep conflicts. But it won't clarify the vision, prioritize actions, or help accelerate the innovation process. And in the end, this means that it won't help you fulfill your mission and calling.

WIDELY KNOWN

A second trait of a powerful mission statement is that it's widely known. Even if it's ruthlessly honest and laser focused, if it's too wordy and complex to remember, it's pretty much useless. To impact the daily decisions of an organization, a mission statement must be easily remembered and repeated ad nauseam — and then repeated again.

When a mission statement is so complex and wordy that no one remembers what it says without stopping to reread it, there's not much chance that daily decisions will be made in light of it or even align with it. Too long to remember is too long to be useful.

Not long ago I came across the mission statement of a prestigious college. It was five paragraphs long. I guarantee you that nobody (even the president) can recite it from memory. And while a five-paragraph mission statement is obviously an extreme example, I find that many statements that are far shorter are still too long and complex to be easily remembered (and thus widely known). Even some shorter statements suffer because they are awkwardly worded and badly in need of some wordsmithing to make them more memorable.

Here's a simple test. If your mission statement is too wordy or complex for *everyone* on your team to remember it without looking it up, it can't bring clarity and focus to their daily decisions. And without a clear understanding of where the bull's-eye lies, there's no way for you or those on your team to know which ideas or innovations have the potential to take you closer to your goal and which ones are merely great ideas that are likely to sidetrack the pursuit of your goals.

Even a pithy and well-worded mission statement needs to be repeated ad nauseam if it's going to be widely known. Unless your team is static and never adds anyone new to the mix, you'll have to risk boring some of the old-timers to make sure the newbies get it.

Since most leaders hate to bore anyone (or worse, be mocked behind their backs), they fail to turn their mission statement into a worn-out mantra. They look around the room and see the team members who have been there forever, and wrongly assume that everyone has heard it enough.

But a great mission statement is like an old saying your dad or your favorite mentor used to say until you were sick of hearing it. Yet now you find yourself using that same saying to guide your life decisions, and you catch yourself passing it on to your own children so often that they too are sick of hearing it.

If you know your mission, make sure it's clearly worded. Then say it, print it, and post it every chance you get. And then do it some more.

BROADLY ACCEPTED

The last trait of a great mission statement is that it's broadly accepted.

There's an old adage that "the policies down the hall always trump the vision on the wall." It's true. Pockets of people or departments within an organization that don't fully buy into the mission, or worse, have a different mission, create confusion and conflict. They also tend to sabotage innovation because their infighting and turf protection inevitably amplifies the natural resistance that most people and organizations have toward change.

In the early days of a church plant or startup, it's easy to gain broad acceptance of your mission. If it's genuine and clearly stated, you'll attract people who agree with it and you will repel those who don't. That's why so many startup teams have a Camelot-like sense of unity.

But it's difficult to maintain that sense of unity and broad acceptance of the mission over time. As organizations grow and mature, there's almost always some measure of mission creep. It's inevitable. New staff and new leaders subtly redefine the mission in terms of their personal perspectives and preferences or the position they have within the organization. And those subtle shifts add up. Eventually, many organizations end up with competing silos, each with a slightly different agenda, and each one duking it out with the others for power, prestige, and resources.

The only way to avoid this is if someone has the authority and guts to step up and periodically recalibrate the vision or realign the organization and its structures with the vision. That's easier said than done. Any attempt at realignment will cause those who are out of alignment to lose some (or all) of their power and prestige. Most people won't give these up easily. Some will fight you to the death.

It's here that an honest and widely known mission statement comes to the rescue. It smokes out those who have a different target. When your bull's-eye is clearly marked and widely known, there's no way for those who insist on aiming at something different to hide. It's obvious to all when they have a different target and a different agenda.

Imagine for a moment that you are a world-class mountain climber. There are lots of challenging and worthy peaks you could choose from. But an expedition can ascend only one peak at a time. To make it to the top, everyone has to agree that this is the peak we're climbing. If someone wants to scale another peak, they need to move on or be left behind.

And it's not only the selection of the mountain peak that demands agreement. You'll also have to agree on the route. There are multiple routes to the top of most mountains. But an expedition has to choose one route and stick to it. There's no room for someone on the team to decide that another route is safer, faster, or easier. To do so would put the whole expedition at risk.

It's the same for a ministry, nonprofit, or business. Those with a different vision need to move on, be left behind, or be asked to leave. This doesn't mean they're bad people. It simply means they're wrong for this team.

The same holds true for those who agree with the vision but want to take a different route. They also need to move on, be left behind, or be asked to leave.

Difficult missions demand laserlike focus. Everyone must agree on the peak you're ascending and the route you're taking. Otherwise you'll have little to no chance of success.

WHY A GREAT MISSION STATEMENT ACCELERATES INNOVATION

When your mission statement is an honest reflection of your passion, is widely known, and is broadly accepted, it will not only help you get where you want to go; it will accelerate innovation. That's because when you have an obvious goal, it becomes clear which ideas and innovations will help propel you toward that goal and which are merely great ideas that won't impact your goal and mission in any significant way.

In other words, a clear and memorable mission statement will tell you what to feed and what to starve, what to focus on and what to ignore. It will give you a framework by which to judge success and failure.

Without missional clarity, it's easy to be seduced by every innovative idea or proposal that appears. Especially if something is novel, has been successful elsewhere, or promises to make a solid short-term profit. But over the long haul, if something doesn't take us toward our mission, it takes us away from our mission, even if it's a great idea and a potential game-changing innovation elsewhere.

· ● ·

It's hard to hit the bull's-eye when it's a moving target or when everyone thinks it's a different target or when no one knows for sure what the target is. But thankfully, that ceases to be a problem when your goal—your mission statement—is ruthlessly honest, widely known, and broadly accepted.

So here's an exercise to help you and your team evaluate your mission statement (assuming you have one) in terms of its honesty, breadth of awareness, and level of acceptance.

Write down your mission statement. Now answer the following questions individually, then as a group:

1. Is this an honest reflection of our genuine passions?
2. Does it include anything that reflects political correctness more than honest passion?
3. Is our mission statement simple enough to be easily remembered?
4. Can our leadership team quote it without looking it up?
5. Can our staff, members, or customers quote it without looking it up?
6. Is our mission statement broadly accepted throughout the organization?
7. Do we have any policies in place that run counter to our mission? List them.
8. Are there any key players or departments that have a different mission or that don't buy into our mission? What are the "elephants in the room"?
9. What (if anything) do we need to change to make our mission statement more ruthlessly honest, widely known, or broadly accepted?

A BIAS FOR ACTION

Why Data and Proof Are Overrated

I'm fond of reminding people that God's will has three components: a what, a when, and a how. Each is equally important. Two out of three won't cut it. Miss out on any of the three and you'll end up in deep weeds.

The same holds true for change and innovation. If the what is a great idea, then the when is right timing and the how is proper execution.

Introduce an innovation too early and it can't take hold, no matter how brilliant the idea may be. Think of Leonardo da Vinci's concepts of manned flight. Without a reliable and adequate source of power to propel his theoretical concepts, there was no way to get his drawings off the ground. His ideas for a helicopter and a hang glider were ingenious. But they were also four centuries ahead of schedule.

It's also possible for a change or innovation to be too late to the party. Imagine coming up with a faster, longer-range, and cheaper dirigible. That idea would have made you lots of money in the early years of the twentieth century. Today, one hundred years later, you'd go broke. No one wants a faster and better blimp anymore.

It's not just timing that determines the fate of a new idea. It's also the implementation process. If we bungle it, even the best of ideas can be dead on arrival. Consider once more the work of Thomas

Edison. He made the lion's share of his profits from the incandescent lightbulb. Yet most of the patents for his lightbulb belonged to other people. They had great ideas and impeccable timing. But they couldn't find a way to bring their lightbulbs to market. They failed the implementation test. So Edison got all the fame and made all the money.

The same thing still happens today. It's not always the best idea that succeeds. It's the combination of a great idea, proper timing, and excellent execution that brings success.

This explains why a strong organizational bias for action is so important. It speeds up the innovation process by quickly moving ideas from the realm of theory into the bright light of reality, where it's easy to see what actually works and what doesn't.

FINDING A WAY TO SAY YES

A bias for action begins by conquering the fear of failure. Leaders and organizations with an inordinate fear of failure have an insatiable appetite for more data and proof. They always want more evidence, more justification for their actions. They won't try anything until all the risk has been wrung out of the equation (or until someone else brings it to market and proves that the idea does, after all, have merit).

A bias for action doesn't imply taking stupid risks that are potentially catastrophic or fatal to the organization. Only a fool does that. It doesn't mean going off half-cocked, betting the farm, or hotly pursuing every new idea that comes our way. It simply means that when presented with a new idea or proposal, we seek to find a way to try it out rather than write it off. We look as hard as we can for a way to say yes.

The only way to determine if an idea has merit is to put it to a test. That's why leaders and organizations with a bias for action are always experimenting at the fringe.

For example, consider Fred DeLuca, the cofounder of Subway. He built a local option into his franchising system. This allowed local owners to experiment with different menu items and marketing ideas. When the owners of two small shops in Miami decided to increase their dismal weekend sales by offering Subway's Footlong sandwiches for only five dollars, weekend sales weren't so dismal anymore. There suddenly were long lines waiting out the door.

It didn't take long for corporate headquarters to figure out that whatever was creating the long lines in Miami could easily translate into increased sales in New Jersey. So they rolled out the Footlong campaign nationwide. Subway sales increased dramatically.

This never could have happened in many other franchising systems. They control everything to the point that no one can experiment at the fringe. But freedom to experiment at the fringe was built into the structure of Mr. DeLuca's franchises, and he and his franchisees have profited handsomely from it.

SOME FAILURES ARE VICTORIES

A bias for action also allows you to discover more quickly what to pursue and what to abandon. This is important, because what brings success to one organization can bring chaos to another.

For instance, I think of two churches that were struggling to retain young families while reaching out to new people in the community. Both of these churches had seen better days, but they were far from finished. They also shared a bias for action rather than a tendency toward paralyzing further study.

When their youth pastors asked for permission to try out an alternative worship service aimed at a younger demographic, both of these churches found a way to say yes. They each offered their gyms and spent money to fix the acoustics and provide decent sound systems.

At one church, the alternative service grew quickly. Five years later, it was much larger than the traditional service (which most people now considered to be the "alternative" service). At the other church, the new service never took off. Today, it still languishes as a small "alternative" worship experience for the "young folks."

Yet—don't miss this—both churches benefited greatly from their bias for action.

The first church discovered that they were more ready for change than anyone thought, and they were able to reach far more people because of it. The second church discovered they weren't ready. But thanks to their bias for action and willingness to experiment at the fringe, they learned this the easy way. Their experiment spared them the heartache that would have come with a failed attempt at a churchwide transition to a more cutting-edge and youthful worship experience.

As we've already seen, there is never enough evidence ahead of time to know with certainty which ideas will succeed and which ones will fail. Before an idea has been tested, the best we have is an educated guess. That's why an exit strategy is always so important, and why the endless pursuit for more data and absolute proof is always futile.

It's always far better to simply try things and then respond to what happens. If it works, look closer and try it again. If it doesn't, move on to something else.

SURPRISED BY SUCCESS: THE BEAUTY OF A FREE LOOK

Another benefit of having a bias for action (and one of the main reasons it accelerates innovation) is that it can provide you with a free look at ideas that otherwise might not get a shot. Without the constraints of endless research, mounds of data, and the need for irrefutable proof, you can quickly try things you think might work—but even better, you can try things you're pretty sure *won't* work, just in case you are wrong.

Here are two examples (one a rather small risk and the other quite large).

Drums in the Sanctuary

Believe it or not, there was a time when bringing drums into a church sanctuary was a risky endeavor. I remember as a young pastor thinking that we needed to push the envelope, musically, if we wanted to reach my own generation. But I was also afraid that I might be martyred in the process.

Though it seems a rather obvious thing to do today, at that time, few churches were willing to make changes to their music style. Those that did were considered liberal.

To get us where we needed to go, I tasked another staff member with aligning our worship services so that the music style matched the current decade. I told him that I had no interest in becoming a historical preservation society.

I knew it would take us a few years to change. But I also knew that we'd inevitably get there once we started down the path. My biggest concern was moving too fast. I didn't want to create a congregational backlash that would send us back to square one. And frankly, I was right to have that concern, because a few years later, worship wars began to spread across the church landscape like wildfire.

One Sunday, long before I thought we were ready, I walked into the church and saw a drum set on the platform. I turned to our worship leader and said, "So you think we're ready for this?"

He said, "Yes."

I thought, You're crazy. There's no way we're ready.

But I *said*, "That's what I hired you for." Then I went into my office and started praying like mad.

Why did I let him go ahead when I was so sure he was wrong?

Because I had a strong bias to say yes. And I also had an exit strategy that had instantly popped into my mind. I figured that if we weren't ready, I'd apologize and the drums would be gone the next week. I knew I already had enough chips in the relational bank that a humble apology and quick action might actually gain me more chips. So why not give it a try?

To my surprise, I was wrong. Our congregation was more than ready for the change. One old codger got up and stormed out of the service. But everyone else was positive or neutral. As for the old guy, he'd been a chronic complainer for a long time. I'd been praying that Jesus would move him out. I didn't realize that Jesus was just waiting for me to let the drums show up.

The upside of that small decision was huge. It opened the door to many other changes and solidified our commitment to think like missionaries, never changing our message but always adapting our methods, style, and cultural language in ways that allowed us to stay relevant in the hyperchanging world of Southern California.

The Church Has Left the Building

We took a much bigger risk on the weekend we decided to close down all of our worship services. We wanted to cancel church for the weekend and send our entire congregation out to serve in a massive community-service project. We called it the Weekend of Service.

We had no idea whether it would work.

Our goal was to mobilize thousands of our congregation to fix up and repair schools, community centers, and dilapidated buildings in the community. We're not talking small projects here; these were extreme makeovers, all to be completed within forty-eight hours.

We knew it would take a ton of people, money, and energy. We knew that if it worked, it would have a major impact on our community and congregation. We also knew that if it didn't work, we'd have some major egg on our faces, both in the community and in our congregation.

We knew of several smaller churches that had pulled off large-scale service projects on a Saturday. We even knew of a few that had closed down for the entire weekend. But we knew of no other mega-church that had shut down *all* of its weekend services in this way.

Large regional churches like ours are a different breed. Some people travel great distances to attend. Outside of the people you know in your small group, there's lots of anonymity. We wondered whether people would actually show up. After all, the conventional criticism of megachurches is that they're filled with "consumer Christians" who come for what they can get, not what they can give.

And what about the offerings? Like most churches and nonprofits, we weren't sitting on a ton of cash. The materials and supplies alone would cost a fortune. They'd have to be paid for up front. We'd lose an entire weekend's worth of offerings if we did this.

Despite these questions and concerns, we decided to go forward. We pulled the trigger.

On the one hand, the risk of failure was real. But it wasn't cat-astrophic. Yes, we could lose face with the congregation and the organizations we planned to help. Yes, we could lose money and have to make some significant programing cuts to make up for it. But there was no threat of a mass exodus. If things went south, we could simply relegate the Weekend of Service to another in a long list of one-time events and move on.

On the other hand, the potential upside was enormous. We were looking for a way to elevate community service to the level of a core value in our church, something that was not true at the time. We dreamed of a church culture in which community service events took place daily.

We even talked about pulling off massive Weekend of Service projects every twelve to eighteen months. But we kept all that to ourselves. Instead of marketing it as the watershed event we hoped it would be, we marketed it as a onetime event, using the language of experimentation, just in case our dream turned out to be a nightmare.

When the weekend finally came, nothing went as expected. Everything far exceeded even our wildest dreams. More than 5,400 of our members showed up. They were amped and ready to serve. They completed ninety-two projects in fifty-six locations. At the end of the forty-eight hours, they had provided our surrounding communities with more than a million dollars in biddable goods and services (and that didn't include any monetary value for the man hours provided).

Now, years later, our Weekends of Service have become signature events with over 10,000 of our members participating. Each time, the number of workers and projects has increased significantly. Better yet, we've been able to create a culture of service and generosity that now averages more than two community service projects per day in addition to our massive Weekends of Service.

Whether it's drums in the sanctuary or a Weekend of Service, a bias for action will accelerate the process of change and innovation within your organization. It will allow you to try things before all the facts are in. It will free you to take measured risks, set you up to survive failure, and occasionally surprise you with successes you never expected.

THE ONE TIME WHEN MORE DATA AND PROOF ARE ALWAYS WARRANTED

There is, however, a time when further study and certainty are warranted. Whenever failure could be fatal to the organization or to the credibility of your leadership team, it's wise to have as many facts as possible before acting.

Consider NASA's manned space flight program. NASA had a long history of incredible innovation with amazing feats of engineering and technological advance. Yet NASA also had an entrenched culture of further study. Everything had to be backed up by a study or a test. In fact, mission control once had a sign that read, "In God we trust. All others bring data."

NASA's mission—and the cargo it carried (human lives)—left it with no other choice. It had to insist on further study and irrefutable proof. When it comes to space exploration, a failure costs lives. There can be absolutely no tolerance for it. And while only a few tragedies ever occurred in NASA's history, each of them is deeply etched into our national consciousness.

NASA never had the luxury of trying lots of things to see what worked. Yes, they experimented. And they did so a lot. But it was always far outside the mission, in a way that didn't put human lives at risk. The cost of failure at the core of the mission was too great to risk.

But let's be real. Most of us aren't risking lives when we fail. We're merely risking time, money, and a measure of our leadership credibility. And at that point, a bias for action will always beat a bias for further study and irrefutable proof that something will succeed.

The fact is, great teams *ship*. They get to market when others are still figuring out if there's a market or where the market is. They know that innovation needs action. And they know that inaction because of an excessive aversion to risk eventually becomes an unintended aversion to success and innovation.

Chapter 9

A RESPECTED CHAMPION

The Difference a John the Baptist Makes

When a leader with long tenure and lots of chips in the bank supports a new idea, its odds of gaining a fair hearing sky-rocket. So do its odds of success.

But what happens if you don't have much tenure or a pile of chips in the bank? What if you're the new kid on the block? What if you're stuck in the middle of the food chain? What if you're at the top, but facing significant pockets of resistance from people who think you shouldn't be at the top?

Does that mean innovation and needed changes have to wait as you gain respectability and credibility? Must it be left for others?

Not at all.

Certainly it will be harder to pull off. But it's not impossible.

The key is to find the people in your organization who have the tenure or the chips to make a difference, and then enlist them for the cause. Because no innovation or significant change ever succeeds without a respected champion.

THE POWER OF A RESPECTED CHAMPION

As we saw earlier, every organization has a natural, knee-jerk resistance to change. It's human nature. Whenever we are presented with any kind of change, most of us immediately focus on what we might lose, especially in terms of power, prestige, and preference.

We don't start out asking, "How will this impact our mission?"

We immediately think, "How will this impact me?"

That's where a respected champion comes into play. A respected champion has a unique ability to calm the troops, reframe the dialogue, and minimize resistance because of his or her wealth of credibility and trust. When a respected champion speaks, people listen. They may still have qualms about the proposed changes, but most folks will give a respected champion the benefit of the doubt. They'll support (or at least stop resisting) whatever he or she supports.

I learned this lesson in the early years of my ministry. I was facing strong opposition to some much needed changes. People started leaving the church, questioning my motives, and assailing my judgment. At one point, it got so bad that I lay awake at night wondering whether the board was going to fire me.

I had zero chips in the bank. Not only was I new to the church; I was new to the job. I'd never been a senior pastor before. I was twenty-eight years old. I was the antithesis of a respected champion.

To make matters worse, I was under the false impression that good ideas should stand on their own. I didn't realize that having a respected champion is just as important as having a great idea, that the credibility of the spokesman can be more important than the validity of the message.

During one particularly difficult time, my mentor showed up. He was a highly esteemed sage, revered for his years of service, and considered by all to be a man of peculiar wisdom and insight. He met with a couple of board members who had become increasingly resistant to my leadership and ideas. They were old enough to be my father, successful in their chosen careers, unsure of my long-term commitment to the church, and certain that I was pushing things too hard, too fast.

At one point, my mentor asked me to explain all the changes I wanted to make and why I thought they were so important. After I'd finished, he said, "I think Larry's right. You ought to do these things. He's got a lot of ideas worth considering. Listen to him."

Bam. Everything changed.

After a little more discussion, the two board members not only green-lighted the changes I wanted to make; they publically supported them.

It was all a bit mind-boggling.

After all, nothing had changed. My proposals were exactly the same. They hadn't been retooled, restated, or implemented differently. The only difference was that now I had the support of a respected champion.

I have never forgotten that lesson. From that day on, I've made it a priority to identify a respected champion before proposing any kind of significant change or innovation. It doesn't matter if I have the best idea since flushed toilets; without a respected champion supporting it, I won't move forward.

After decades of ministry at North Coast, I now have the tenure and chips to qualify as a respected champion. But I still look to others. While it's true that you can have only one champion in the ring, when it comes to innovation and significant change, you can never have too many champions for the cause.

HOW TO FIND AND RECRUIT A RESPECTED CHAMPION

It's easy to identify the respected champions within your organization. Simply ask, "Who are the people who can singlehandedly kill an idea by their opposition, and who are the people who can make it fly with their support?"

These are your power brokers and your potential respected champions.

It doesn't matter whether they have an official title or position within your organization. They often don't. But they have something far more important. They have the ears of the people.

Once you've identified a potential respected champion, solicit their support *privately*.

Never share your new idea or proposal with a power broker for the first time in a public setting. That's because a public forum is ripe for miscommunication and offers little opportunity to restate or clarify anything that is misunderstood. What we mean to say, what we actually say, and what people hear can be three different things. In a public forum, it's hard to know when and whether these three actually align.

It's much easier to communicate clearly in a one-on-one setting. Initial hesitation or resistance is hard to hide. You can ask questions. If you misspoke, you can restate the proposal. If you've been misunderstood, you can clarify. If you need to make some tweaks to gain support, you can do so. None of this is possible in a larger setting.

But there is another equally important reason why you don't want a power broker to hear your new idea or proposal for the first time in a group setting. That's because they seldom change their mind once they've gone public with their support or opposition.

I'm not sure why that is. I'm not saying it's a good thing. I'm just pointing out how life works. Public figures, leaders, and power brokers may change their minds a lot behind the scenes, but they seldom do so once they've gone public.

That's why I make sure I always talk to them in an informal setting, presenting my ideas as a first draft, not a final proposal. It gives me lots of wiggle room to fine-tune, restate the idea in a better way, or even make some major changes to gain their support.

I've found that initial opposition often turns to enthusiastic support once we've had the time to dialogue. A one-on-one setting helps clear up the misunderstandings that are inherent in trying to explain an idea that hasn't been tried yet or an innovation that doesn't exist yet. All it usually takes is a listening ear and a willingness to make some minor changes.

Now, obviously, not everyone is convinced after a one-on-one meeting. Sometimes a power broker will hate your idea no matter how many ways you restate it or how many tweaks you offer to make. Their opposition is not a matter of poor communication; it's a matter of differing viewpoints.

On the surface, it may seem like that kind of preliminary meeting would only make matters worse by giving a potential opponent more time and extra ammo to torpedo your idea. While that could happen theoretically, I've never seen it or experienced it firsthand. In fact, I've found the opposite to be true. I've found that the respect that comes from personally seeking out the unofficial and official leaders ahead of time for a one-on-one meeting tends to temper their opposition. Typically, people don't fight dirty with people they like, even when they strongly disagree.

BEYOND THE LAUNCH

So far, we've been talking about the power of a respected champion to help you get a new idea, a major change, or an innovation off the ground. But there is another way that respected champions accelerate successful change and innovation. They provide protective cover during those perilous early days when a major change or innovation has been launched, but has not yet fully taken hold.

Some innovations take off like a rocket. But most don't. Serial innovators know that lots of innovations that look like great successes now, nearly died in infancy. Serial innovators don't give up when the pace of adoption is slower than they had hoped. They realize that innovation isn't just about getting an idea launched. It's about seeing it through until it is fully accepted and widely adopted. And that takes time.

Most people in your organization won't get that. They'll assume that great ideas are immediately and widely adopted. Many of your leaders will panic when they sense the low-level frustration that accompanies any major change. They'll interpret it as a major crisis or a coup waiting to happen. And those who desire harmony above all else will interpret every complaint and criticism they hear as a cry of despair.

All of this is predictable.

Studies show that when major changes or innovations are introduced, only a small percentage of people become early adopters. Most people wait and take their cues from others. They hold back and want to know who else is supporting it before they jump aboard. These are the people who most need a respected champion. Without that champion, many of them are just like the children of Israel, pleading to return to Egypt when the Promised Land doesn't show up as soon as they expected. A respected champion can convince them to stay the course.

Respected champions not only will help you get your great idea off the ground; they also will help keep it in orbit, especially in the early days, when every innovation is vulnerable to the natural resistance that change brings.

WHO'S YOUR "JOHN THE BAPTIST"?

Even Jesus used a respected champion to kick-start his ministry.

His name was John the Baptist.

Jesus recruited his first disciples from the ranks of John's followers. When John told them that Jesus was the one they were looking for, they immediately left John and followed Jesus. No questions asked. No miracles needed.

I figure that if Jesus felt the need for someone like John the Baptist to pave the way and give credibility to his new ministry and teachings, I ought to have someone like that too. That's why, whenever possible, I look for someone with acknowledged credibility and trust to help smooth the way when I'm launching a new program or introducing a new idea. They make a big difference in how people respond.

To identify the potential respected champions within your organization, ask the following questions. They will help you and your team pinpoint those who are most respected, whose words carry weight with others, and whose support will calm the fears of those most resistant to change.

1. Who are the one or two people on the leadership team or board who have the power to kill an idea with their opposition even if they are the only ones strongly against it?
2. Who are the key people in your organization who don't hold an official position or title but have enough relational capital to singlehandedly derail or accelerate the success of a new program or idea?

3. What weight does tenure carry in your leadership team? What weight does tenure carry in your organization?

4. Who has enough tenure to determine the success or failure of a proposal?

5. Who are the two or three people your longtime folks are most apt to listen to?

6. Who are the two or three people your newer folks are most apt to listen to?

7. If these names are different, what significance does that have? What should be done about it?

PLANNING IN PENCIL

Letting an Innovation Be What It Wants to Be

Successful changes and innovations tend to take on lives of their own. They seldom end up exactly where or what their creators thought they would be.

German chemist Alfred Einhorn was seeking to invent a nonaddictive narcotic for general surgery. In 1905, he succeeded in inventing what we now call Novocain. To his chagrin, his invention was rejected by most surgeons because they favored general anesthesia, while dentists loved the new drug, using it to help them pull teeth. Einhorn was convinced that dentists' use of Novocain *devalued* his noble invention and undercut its potential market for general surgery. So he spent the later part of his life in a fruitless attempt at keeping dentists from using it.[8]

Clearly, he didn't have much success. And in hindsight, we can't help but wonder, "What was he thinking?"

Thomas Edison had a similar experience. He envisioned his invention of the phonograph as a business tool that could be used for dictation. He had no idea that the technology behind it would eventually launch a massive music industry. He actually put the newly invented phonograph aside to work on other projects. Despite his brilliance as a market-oriented inventor, he couldn't see the gold mine that his invention would eventually open.

Or, more recently, consider the story of Dr. Spencer Silver, creator of the glue that makes Post-It Notes possible. Dr. Silver was an employee of 3M. He was attempting to formulate a powerful glue when he ended up creating a low-tack, pressure-sensitive, reusable glue. Having no idea what it was good for, he tried to promote it to the management of 3M to see if they had any ideas on how it could be used. They labeled it a solution without a problem.

Six years later, one of Dr. Silver's coworkers started using it to temporarily hold a bookmark in his hymnbook. It worked marvelously. So Dr. Silver put some of it on the back side of a pad of paper, and suddenly, Dr. Silver's solution had found its problem.[9]

It makes you wonder how the brilliant and innovative minds at 3M missed this obvious application. When presented with the low-tack glue Dr. Silver had invented, they saw what is now a hot-selling product as nothing more than "a solution without a problem."

This should remind us of the truth that we don't really know what something is—whether it's a new product, a new program, or some other innovation—until it hits the real world. Only then do we know what we have on our hands. Until then, it's just a concept or a theory. Only after it has been released into the wild can we know how it will actually work, how people will respond to it, and what *it* wants to be.

That's why we should always plan and innovate in pencil. And not just at the beginning, when we're coming up with new and creative ideas. Use a pencil all the way through the lifecycle, making plans, but always being ready to change them at a moment's notice.

PLANNING IN PENCIL

Planning in pencil simply means keeping your options open as long as possible. It involves using the language of flexibility rather than certainty. It's being careful to say, "This is what we do for now," rather than, "This is what we will do forever." It's making sure that everyone knows that midcourse corrections aren't simply allowed; they're encouraged.

Let's say that you're launching a major new program. Obviously you have to start with a schedule, a location, a time frame, a curriculum, and standards. But once you launch, it's certain that the schedule, location, time frame, curriculum, and standards you set will need to be fine-tuned. Nothing ever works as planned. It's likely that these things will need a major overhaul. It all depends on how the real world and the marketplace respond.

Let's look at some examples of how things change and why planning and innovating in pencil is so important.

A Lecture-Lab Church

At North Coast Church, our entire ministry is built around sermon-based small groups. Think "lecture-lab," with the weekend sermon being the lecture and the weekly small group being the lab. When we launched the concept nearly thirty years ago, we knew of no other churches using our model. (There might have been, we just didn't know of any.) It was an innovative and laser-focused paradigm.

These midweek small groups have been a smashing success from day one. Our weekly small group attendance has always exceeded 80 percent of our weekend attendance. Currently, it's more than 90 percent. These groups have helped slam our back door shut. They've turned a massive crowd into a church. They've been the major reason for our sustained growth and spiritual health over the years.

Yet we've constantly had to tweak them. Even from the beginning, nothing has gone exactly as planned.

We thought leaders wanted and needed lots of training. So we not only offered it; we made it mandatory. Until we realized that some of our best leaders were the ones who skipped the extra meetings.

We thought we could make every group sermon-based. But we quickly realized that if you treat adults like children, they don't respond too well. So we stepped back and started allowing groups to pick a different type of Bible study for a quarter, as long as they returned to our sermon-based curriculum when the quarter was over.

We imagined leaders would prepare for their groups by listening to a weekly fifteen-to-twenty-minute training tape. (This was before everyone had internet access.) But our leaders weren't sitting down at the kitchen table to listen with pen, paper, and Bible in hand. They were listening to the training in their car—on the day of the meeting, often on their way to the meeting.

We also envisioned tiered layers of oversight, with each group overseen by a volunteer leader of five groups, who would be overseen by a leader of twenty-five groups. With this limited span of care (no one directly overseeing more than five people), we were sure we had the ideal administrative and coaching system in place. It was manageable and realistic. It looked great on paper.

It sucked in real life. The volunteers hated it.

And then there was our neighborhood focus. We imagined that people preferred to be grouped by neighborhood. But we hadn't realized that in Southern California, the neighborhood is no longer a useful construct. Nobody identifies themselves by their neighborhood unless it's a new housing tract. The new neighborhoods are our workplaces, our station in life, and our special interests. So we had to reengineer our groups in light of that reality.

I could go on. After nearly thirty years, the list of things we've been wrong about or radically changed is quite long. But we've continued to be successful because we've been willing to change as the facts changed. And to do so quickly.

Coffee Snobs

The story of Starbucks provides another illustration of how important it is to plan in pencil. Prior to the rise of Starbucks, you would have been hard-pressed to find anyone in America who believed that selling premium coffee at premium prices was a viable business model. For most people, coffee was a commodity, and many preferred the convenience of instant coffee heated up in a microwave over the time and hassle it took to brew a fresh pot.

Starbucks changed everything. But one of the major reasons why Starbucks was so successful changing America was that it also let America change Starbucks.

In his book *Pour Your Heart into It*, Howard Schultz tells the fascinating story of Starbucks' innovative rise to become one of America's premier brands. It's a story full of midcourse corrections.

And it's quite clear that the outcome would have been radically different had Schultz written down the details of his original dream in permanent ink instead of in pencil.

For instance, Schultz and his early management team had a passion for quality coffee and wanted to instill that passion in others. So they started out with a long list of things they would *never* do.

That list included never franchising, avoiding supermarkets, and never letting their coffee be served in settings they couldn't control (such as in a Marriott or on a United Airlines flight). They also determined that they would never sell flavored coffee or add flavored syrups to a latte. Nonfat lattes also were taboo, because Italian espresso bars use whole milk. As for foo-foo drinks like a Frappuccino, there was no way they'd even consider such a thing.[10]

Obviously, they've made a few midcourse corrections. Try to imagine Starbucks with a CEO unwilling to have made those changes. It would have produced a different niche brand, with a very different stock price.

Video Venues

The same thing happened when we introduced the video venues that I mentioned earlier. When I first came up with the idea, I thought it would be a great way to turn an overflow room into a reward instead of a punishment. I also saw it as a great way to broaden our demographic outreach. By offering different worship styles, I figured we could reach people we'd never reach with our old one-size-fits-all style of worship. I even saw it as a great way for a bigger church to feel like a smaller church and to avoid having to build a massive sanctuary.

But I missed out on one of the most important uses of a video venue. I failed to see that it could also be a powerful tool for launching satellite campuses and for beginning a multisite ministry.

In fact, when our executive pastor, Charlie Bradshaw, first suggested that we use our venues in this way, I blew him off. I told him that it wouldn't work. I couldn't imagine putting together all of the ministries that a stand-alone church would need for an off-site video venue. And if we did this, who would come?

But it wasn't too long before a handful of churches who had come to see what we were doing took our new toy and started to play with it in the wrong way. Instead of creating on-site venues to reach a broader demographic audience, they planted satellite campuses to reach a wider geographic audience. Only then did I realize that our video venues had far more potential than I had envisioned. So we started launching our own satellite campuses, and pretended that we had planned to do so all along.

I share this to illustrate a common problem: innovators sometimes see the trajectory of their innovations so clearly that they have a hard time recognizing new opportunities when their innovations veer off course and go in their own directions. Even worse, they tend to fight it.

STAYING FLEXIBLE

The best way to keep this from happening is to plan and proceed in pencil. Throw away the pen. Never use it. Even mature innovations need tweaks and an occasional overhaul.

The only thing you and your leadership team can know for sure about the future is that it will be different from what you think it will be. So prepare for it by keeping as many options open as long as possible.

Avoid instituting game plans that are so detailed there's no room for adjustment.

Never fall in love with your first draft—or your latest draft.

Institute guiding principles instead of rigid policies.

Always keep your ear to the ground. Things change when you least expect it.

And never forget that successful and serial innovators deal with what is. They don't worry much about what should be. They don't worry much about what they thought would be. They just worry about what is. And when things change, they change.

Part Four

SABOTAGING INNOVATION

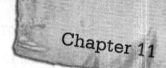

Chapter 11

THE HIGH PRICE OF FAILURE

Why Trust and Credibility Are Too Important to Lose

Americans love redemption stories. We love tales of rags to riches, of people overcoming terrible tragedies and crushing failures to reach the heights of success. We love the second-chance, I'll-prove-you-wrong storyline.

Chances are you've heard of Abraham Lincoln's countless lost elections, or that Albert Einstein was told he was stupid for years, or how Michael Jordon was cut from his high school basketball team, or how Fred Smith's business school professor gave him a C because his concept of a national delivery service (the one we now know as FedEx) had zero chance of succeeding. All of these stories are widely told. They reassure us that our own stumbles and failures don't have to be final.

I suppose that's a good thing. After all, these stories are true. And failure can be a great teacher, a springboard to success. Why not encourage people who are about to throw in the towel? Why not inspire them to keep going, never to quit?

But the fact is some failures *are* final. It doesn't matter how much we believe in ourselves or how doggedly we pursue the dream, some failures permanently close the door. They slam it shut, even if we won't admit it and refuse to give up.

I think of Darren. He once made a terrible decision and got behind the wheel after drinking too much at a friend's bachelor party. He ran through a red light and broadsided a family's sedan, killing a young mom and her daughter.

If you met Darren today, you'd be impressed. He'd strike you as a responsible, caring, and upstanding citizen. He's become a committed Christian, carefully aligning his life with Jesus' teachings. He's a youth leader at his church.

But no matter how long he continues to take the right path or how much water flows under the bridge, there are some places Darren will never be able to go. He's a convicted felon. He'll never vote. He'll never live out his boyhood dream of being a peace officer. He'll never be able to pursue employment in a number of licensed professions. Blood on your hands and three years in prison will do that to you.

I tell Darren's story to illustrate an important point. Not all failures are equal. Some are far worse than others. Some are impossible to recover from.

If you're a leader, you can't avoid failure. It comes with the territory. You'll make bad decisions because you failed to size up the situation accurately. You'll even make some right decisions, only to watch circumstances that are out of your control turn them into the wrong decisions. You'll hire people you should have passed on, trust folks who prove untrustworthy, and launch programs and products that are dead on arrival.

All of these are normal leadership failures. They can be overcome. But other kinds of leadership failures are nearly impossible to overcome. You'll want to avoid them at all costs. I call them "leadership felonies."

LEADERSHIP FELONIES

The first and worst leadership felony is any kind of moral failure. We expect smart people to do dumb things occasionally. But we expect that honest people will always be honest, and that moral people will always be moral. Leaders who lie, cheat, break promises, or reveal the moral bankruptcy of their character have generally reached the end of their leadership road. Failure of this sort destroys the primary currency of leadership: trust and credibility. Without them, a leader can't do much.

But a moral failure is not the only kind of felony a leader can commit. Several other leadership felonies are equally debilitating. They aren't as spectacular or shameful as a public moral failure. But they can be just as damaging to a leader's ability to lead, innovate, or make necessary changes within an organization. They occur whenever our failures are (1) high profile, (2) overhyped, or (3) repeatedly made.

THE SPOTLIGHT'S CURSE

Now, you might be thinking, wait a minute, aren't there lots of leaders with a long list of failures *before* they finally succeeded?

The answer is yes.

But if you look closely, you'll realize that their early failures were anything but high profile. In virtually every case, they occurred in relative obscurity. And keep in mind that their failures *preceded* their fame. The only people impacted were friends, family, and a few investors.

Your favorite entrepreneur may have flunked out of college and struggled through a couple of failed startups. But it's only now that he's rich and famous, bequeathing large sums of money to charity and serving on the board of the college he flunked out of, that you hear about it. It's old news.

The same for the high-profile pastor who credits his early failures as the key to his success. We hear about his failures from the main stage of the big conference he's speaking at or the bestselling book he's written. At that point, they're far away in the past, now known by many, but actually experienced by few.

Those kinds of low-profile failures are easy to overcome. In fact, letting people in on them can add to your street cred once you've succeeded. It paints an image of vulnerability and humility.

But let those same failures happen under the glare of the spotlight, and the response of the crowd will be different. It's one thing to learn some tough financial lessons when your small startup runs out of cash. It's another thing when you're the leader of a publicly traded company that goes bankrupt, or a cash-starved business that implodes under the weight of too many receivables, or a church that goes broke because you convinced everyone that "if we build it, they will come," and no one came.

These kinds of high-profile failures won't prepare you for the future. They'll destroy your future, because they squander trust and credibility.

Failure may be a great teacher. But make no mistake, its lessons are best learned in a small out-of-the-way classroom.

The high price of high-profile failure illustrates once again the importance of innovating at the fringe, starting out with both a game plan and an exit strategy, and using the language of experimentation whenever possible.

Successful change agents and serial innovators don't mind failing. But they make sure their failures aren't fatal to the trust they've built up over the years. They never confuse high-risk gambling with innovative leadership. They understand the high cost of a high-profile failure.

THE CURSE OF HYPE

Another common leadership felony is the overhyped failure.

If we hype something that succeeds, all is well. But if we hype something that fails, the loss in trust can be significant. And if we hype everything, it won't be long until our words are white noise, the leadership equivalent of a carnival barker.

If your primary goal is to get something off to a great start, hype will work. But if your goal is long-term success (or the chance to try again should this idea not work out so well), hype kills. It, too, undermines trust and credibility.

I grew up in a church where every guest speaker, new program, and special event was marketed as a life-changer you couldn't afford to miss. We all knew it wasn't true. But that didn't stop the people making announcements, printing bulletins, and sending out the newsletter. I'm pretty sure they thought it would increase attendance.

But all it did was fuel cynicism. We all knew from experience that the best thing about these "world class" speakers and missionaries was that they could cure insomnia, usually before they were on to their second point.

Unfortunately, most leaders seem to be drawn to overselling. They want things to start off with a bang. They want results. Right now. So they fall into the hype trap.

But big crowds and enthusiasm aren't worth celebrating if the crowds and enthusiasm quickly wane. It's cause for grave concern. A fast start that quickly fades is a disaster. It means that the word on the street is, "I tried it, and it wasn't very good."

It's far better to start out slow, make adjustments, and build momentum over time. Never forget that people won't judge your church, company, or leadership by how you start out. They will judge it by how you do over the long haul.

That's one reason why I always use as little hype as possible. It occasionally frustrates staff and people who wish I would push a new program, change, or innovation harder. But I won't do it. I want the word on the street to be that everything I push is better than advertised. In the long run, that's the best hype and marketing possible.

Here's just one example of how I've resisted the urge to hype, and the benefits it reaped. It has to do with the way we launched our new main campus after spending nearly twenty years meeting in a converted warehouse.

The standard procedure for a new campus launch is to host a massive grand opening. It usually produces instant growth followed by a slow slide back to a new normal. Lots of pastors seem to see that as a big win. But to my thinking, it's a huge loss when 20 to 30 percent initial growth dwindles to 10 percent actual growth.

So we did something different. Rather than kick off with a hyped-up grand opening, we took our cues from the world of high-end restaurants. We had a soft opening.

A soft opening in the restaurant world means inviting friends and associates to fill the place up so that you can stress-test the waitstaff and kitchen while also evaluating everything on the new menu. It's a great way to discover and fix problems before real customers show up. And it's usually more than a one-night deal. It often lasts a week or two so that *all* of the bugs can be worked out, not just the big and obvious ones.

For us, a soft opening meant absolutely no marketing, advertising, or press releases. Instead of encouraging our congregation to invite their friends, we asked them to hold back. We knew the first few weeks would be a zoo. And they were.

Everything was new to everybody. We had congested parking lots, chaotic classrooms filled with amped-up kids, and gremlins in the sound system. No one had their routine down: where to park, how to drop off their kids, where to find the nearest restroom or grab a cup of coffee, or anything else that they'd previously done on automatic pilot.

All in all, it was no big deal. It was predictable. It was exactly what we expected.

But imagine adding a couple thousand first-time visitors to the mix. That would have been a catastrophe, a guaranteed terrible experience for anyone checking us out to see if we were worth a return visit.

Now, if we'd decided to have a grand opening, I guarantee you that we would have put together an absolutely stunning worship experience and kid's program. From the outside and to our leadership team, it would have looked phenomenal. We would have seen the massive crowds, jam-packed parking lots, sizzling programs and gone home thinking we'd hit a home run. After all, leaders love it when there's standing room only. We see that as a great success. But I'm pretty sure that the people who have to stand don't see it that way.

Grand openings and big campaigns can draw huge crowds. But for most people, they're special events, sort of like annual trips to the county fair. The parking mess, long lines, and anonymous crowds are the price you pay to take your family there. No one complains because it's part of the experience. But few people plan to come back the next week. Most of us wait until next year.

The kinds of people who are looking for a church home are different from the kinds of people who visit on a special occasion. They aren't looking for a sizzling program as much as a place to connect and grow. For most of them, an amazing program can't make up for a multitude of other things that are frustrating, annoying, or awkwardly uncomfortable. It's like going to a restaurant where the steak is phenomenal but the restrooms are filthy, the service slow, and the dishes dirty. Not many of us would venture back, no matter how awesome the filet mignon.

Underhyping our grand opening resulted in much slower initial growth. The first month, we jumped up only a few hundred. But one year later, we'd grown by well over a thousand. Better yet, we didn't have a long list of people who had tried it once when we didn't know what we were doing and decided that they'd never try it again.

Leaders build trust and credibility by constantly underpromising and overdelivering. A pattern of overhyping does the opposite. It undercuts trust, making it nearly impossible to push through major innovation or change, because when it's time to step forward and say, "Trust me on this one," no one does anymore.

THE CURSE OF LEADERSHIP ADHD

A third leadership felony is repeated failure.

I'm not talking here about a history of colossal failures. When it comes to spectacular failure, most leaders and leadership teams never get a second chance. It's one and done. I'm talking about a history of midsized failures, the kind that are most often the result of a bad case of leadership ADHD: lots of things are started and nothing is finished.

We've all seen leaders who can't resist a new idea.

Some are readers. They want to reengineer the entire company every time a new management technique makes the *New York Times* bestsellers list.

Some are conference junkies. They come back from every seminar or conference fired up about a new vision and strategy.

Some are simply manic. They come up with a plethora of ideas all on their own—all at once.

But all of these folks have one thing in common: a tired and confused staff. No one knows what butterfly they're supposed to be chasing.

This type of an-idea-a-minute leadership can be exhilarating initially, especially when a charismatic leader with a gift for selling is at the helm. Such leaders often have an innate ability to make every idea seem like the next big thing. There's never a trace of doubt.

But after awhile, most people figure it out. Instead of charging off to chase the latest butterfly, they feign agreement, but do nothing. They've learned that "this too shall pass." So they keep on doing whatever they were doing before, while the newbies who haven't figured it out yet drop everything to jump on the latest bandwagon.

Once the default response to a new idea becomes "this too will pass," a leader's ability to innovate or implement significant change is pretty much done. When your staff sets up an office pool to see how long this latest idea or program will last, you've become a leader without followers.

Ironically, ADHD leadership is not that far from innovative leadership. It's just a few degrees off. But they are important degrees.

Both try lots of stuff. But innovative leadership tries it in an experimental mode. Nothing is oversold. Everything is subservient to, and judged by, its impact on the mission. (And the mission never changes. No one wonders, "What's really important around here?")

In contrast, leaders with leadership ADHD never slow down to experiment. Every idea that passes through their heads—or that seems to work elsewhere—is pursued full speed ahead. It's the only speed they know. As for the mission, it's ever changing, the only constant being, "Catch *that* butterfly!" at least until a new one comes along.

It's the difference between Jack in the Box and In-N-Out Burger. (Humor me, I live in Southern California, birthplace of the famous In-N-Out chain.)

In-N-Out never changes its menu and seldom advertises. Everyone knows that if you want a great burger, fries, and a drink, head on over to In-N-Out. That's all they do. You can't get a salad. You can't get a taco. But you can get a great burger, fries, and a drink.

Jack, on the other hand, always has a new item on the menu and lots of funny commercials. But he's usually so busy marketing his latest peanut-butter, bacon, and grilled-jalapeno sandwich that he never seems to notice that the cheeseburgers and fries are disgusting.

That's what happens when leadership ADHD takes over. It results in a constant stream of new initiatives and failed projects that eventually numbs everyone to the importance of the core items on the menu.

· ● ·

Any of these three leadership felonies (high-profile failure, over-hyped failure, and repeated failure) will sabotage innovation. That's why a wise leader and leadership team avoid them at all costs.

If you are a leader, there is no way to avoid failure. And there is no way to succeed without trying lots of stuff (much of which won't work). But you can do so without committing any of these leadership felonies if you learn the jujitsu of the serial innovator: always lead with a low-profile experiment, undersell whenever possible, and avoid anything that looks or smells like leadership ADHD.

Chapter 12

GROUPTHINK

Why You Shouldn't Care What Everybody Else Thinks

In the same way that too many cooks spoil the broth, too much input spoils innovation.

Conventional wisdom often suggests the opposite. "If you want better ideas, get as many people involved in the process as possible. The more the merrier, because the key to greater innovation and creativity is greater collaboration."

But that's baloney. It's simply not true.

Remember, successful change agents and serial innovators think differently. They have an eerie ability to mentally model how people will respond. And once they "see the model," they're usually so confident of its clarity and accuracy that they're willing to take what look like great risks based on it. Yet they also will turn on a dime when new information surfaces, morphing and changing the model until their idea succeeds in the real world.

None of this is normal. In fact, it's weird. But it's vital to the innovation process.

Inviting too many people into the innovation or decision-making process waters down the contribution of serial innovators. Their voices become just one of many (and often misunderstood at that). We risk diluting—even drowning out—the valuable counterintuitive insights they bring to the table.

Let's imagine that you are a master chef opening a gourmet

restaurant. You'd want to pull together a creative and enthusiastic team of waiters, bussers, kitchen help, and sous chefs. You might hire an out-of-the-box interior designer, a cutting-edge graphic artist, and a number of other creatives to help you stand out from the crowd. But when it comes to the menu, you don't let any of them decide what to serve or how to cook, season, or present it on the plate.

It's not because you're arrogant. It's because you're a certified master chef and they are not. And while you'd be foolish to ignore others' reactions (what dishes sell well, which ones come back half-eaten, and which ones no one seems to order), at the end of the day, you make the call, because customers don't line up to try the Busboy's Favorite or pay top dollar for the Waiter's Delight.

In the same way, innovators need to be allowed to lead, paying close attention to the feedback of others and the real-world response to their ideas without ceding *control* of the process, final product, or decision to groupthink.

THE PROBLEM WITH GROUPTHINK

The crowd will have its day. Once a new program, product, or major change is introduced, they'll vote with their feet and their wallets. They *always* have the final say.

But crowds aren't very good at envisioning the future, either what could be or should be. They tend to evaluate new ideas and concepts in light of what they already know and experience.

That's why most of my staff thought video venues was a bad idea, nothing but a glorified overflow room. It's also why Swiss watchmakers gave away the technology to the quartz crystal. And why the manufacturers of traditional X-ray technology rejected a prototype of a CT scanner as having no market value. They couldn't envision it becoming a useful or profitable medical device, especially since it originally was cobbled together using pieces of a toy train, a record player, and an alarm clock. So they turned it down.

The main problem with groupthink is not the plethora of opinions and ideas that people bring to the process. That can be a good thing. There's often treasure to be found in the pile. The problem with groupthink is that it tends to succumb to a herd mentality and a desire for harmony. When this tendency takes over, it inevitably sabotages, postpones, or derails innovation and much-needed change long before they can get off the ground.

Here's how.

HERD MENTALITY

A herd mentality is simply our natural inclination to look to others when deciding what to do or how to think. We all take cues from others. It can't be helped. It's how we're wired. Even people who pride themselves on being iconoclastic and ignoring what others think and say have a tribe and a code they carefully conform to. It might be a small tribe, but it's there nonetheless. A genuinely unique rebel is hard to find.

The First to Speak

This tendency toward a herd mentality is a powerful force in most group settings (be it a committee, a task force, a product team, or a Bible study group). Watch what happens after the first person speaks. Whatever they say usually ends up shaping the rest of the conversation. It doesn't matter what others were thinking beforehand; once the first person speaks, everyone else tends to follow their lead and the topic they bring up.

In board meetings or planning sessions, this tendency can sabotage the decision-making process. It allows the most extroverted or negative person to frame the discussion and set the agenda. Whatever issues they raise become the issues that dominate the conversation, even if no one else shared those concerns when they walked into the room.

Conventional Wisdom

Another example of herd mentality at work is the unquestioned authority that we give to conventional wisdom. It, too, can lead to some really bad decisions.

Some conventional wisdom is spot on. That's why it's so widely accepted. It has been proven over time.

But there are also plenty of urban legends that are widely believed but patently false. And they don't just have to do with alligators in the New York sewer system, airheads drying poodles in the microwave, or some crazy guy with a hook sneaking around Lovers' Lane. They also have to do with our day-to-day assumptions about how life works.

Unfortunately, most of our false assumptions are buried deep *within* conventional wisdom. There's no way to know they're false until something happens to expose them. Which explains why *everyone* once believed that bloodletting could cure disease, that the sun revolved around the earth, and that doctors didn't need to bother to sanitize their hands before performing surgery.

It's enough to make me wonder what aspects of today's conventional wisdom will make us look silly and foolish to future generations.

It also explains why committees and focus groups are innovation's worst nightmare. Groups have a hard time escaping the gravitational pull of conventional wisdom. They tend to reject outright anything that doesn't fit their standard paradigm or hasn't been done before. Worse, there's no way to convince them otherwise, since there's no hard evidence to point to when something hasn't yet been done.

It's no wonder that serial innovators generally seek permission to field-test their ideas rather than sell their ideas. They know that it's much easier to get a group to grant them permission to try an idea than it is to get permission to launch an idea. Once their idea has been field-tested, they know they'll have a few facts with which to push back on conventional wisdom. And if the test is successful, they know there's a chance the herd might actually listen to what they have to say.

The Curse of Expertise

It's not just committees and focus groups that succumb to the herd mentality. So do the experts. They have it just as bad as everyone else.

Consider the long list of Nobel Prize winners. It's amazing how many of them had to endure rejection and ridicule from their fellow scientists before their facts finally won the day. You'd think that a group of people who pride themselves on research and hard facts would welcome someone who has new facts for them to consider. But once the experts all agree on something, they're just like the rest of us. They tend to close ranks and listen to one another.

It's easy to see why. Experts rise to prominence by having a deep understanding of their field. They know it inside out. They know what works, what doesn't, and why. They've "seen it all."

But their deep knowledge of the present can blind them to the future. They can be so consumed by what is and has been that they have little bandwidth for what could be. That's why there are so many stories about brilliant leaders ignoring, rejecting, or even giving away the technology and innovations that eventually ate their lunch.

It also explains why a panel of experts can be the death knell for innovation and major change. If an innovation is groundbreaking or paradigm shifting, odds are the experts won't see it as such. Experts tend to see anything in their field that they don't know about as trivial and anything they don't understand as nonsensical. After all, they are the experts.

THE DESIRE FOR HARMONY

Another significant innovation killer is the built-in desire for harmony that most boards, committees, and project groups bring to the process.

Now you might be thinking, "How can that be? Aren't boards, committees, and project groups notorious for conflict?"

Yes, they are.

But their conflict is often rooted in a misguided effort to maintain harmony. They can't make a tough decision and move on. In an effort to find a solution that keeps everyone happy, they keep picking at the scab.

This gives inordinate power to those who are angry or stubborn. All they have to do is blow up or dig in their heels, and most groups will back up and start looking for a compromise. Everyone else in the room may have been ready to sign off and move on. It doesn't matter. The moment that discord arises, most groups immediately will slow down, table, or radically alter whatever it was that caused the stir. They'll let their desire for relational harmony trump making the right decision almost every time.

LOW-LEVEL FRUSTRATION IS NOT MUTINY

Boards, committees, and leadership teams also tend to confuse low-level frustration with mutiny. They worry too much.

There will always be some members who hear isolated complaints or criticisms and extrapolate them into mass dissatisfaction. When they bring their concerns to the leadership team, some folks will panic. They forget that late adopters are never thrilled about any change on the front end, even those that prove to be highly successful and game changing on the back end.

After you've made a significant change, the important question isn't, "Are some people unhappy or mildly frustrated with this change?" The key question is, "Are they leaving or just griping?"

I'm reminded of the time we moved onto our new main campus. It was a massive upgrade. Yet there were plenty of low-level frustrations linked to all the changes that came with it. Hearing lots of complaints, many of our staff members were deeply concerned. They wondered if we had made a huge mistake. They assumed that if we had done things differently or communicated better, everyone would be fine with the new classrooms, chairs, parking, venues, and restroom locations. Some were so concerned that they thought we should halt any further programing changes and send out an all-church letter or hold a special meeting to address the things they heard people complaining about. They feared we were on the cusp of a mass exodus.

But they were wrong. We were simply experiencing the natural pushback that comes with any significant change. For those who liked familiarity, nothing was familiar. For those who liked to gripe, there were lots of new things to gripe about. For those who were late adopters, it was too soon to settle in. None of this was unusual. All of it was predictable.

So I gathered the staff and once again walked them through

research on the diffusion of innovation and how groups process change. We had covered all of this before. But at that time it was mere theory. Now we were in the midst of real-life confusion and discord.

To their credit, they got it. There was *nothing* we could have done that would have turned our late adopters into early adopters. Better communication, or even a redesign of the buildings, wouldn't have changed a thing. There was no silver bullet to make the process painless for everyone. Six months later, the complaints and frustrations had dissipated. We were settled in and moving on.

The fact is, there will always be some level of organizational frustration surrounding any significant innovation or change. Expect it. Embrace it. There's no way around it.

Unfortunately, this is a hard concept to get across to a board, committee, or leadership team. No matter how badly a change might be needed, someone will always want to slow it down, table it, send it out for further study, or alter it beyond recognition in a futile quest for harmony.

Many leadership teams would rather hurt the cause than hurt someone's feelings. Which explains why any innovation or major change that has to pass through a gauntlet of committees or boards seldom escapes unscathed—and often never makes it out alive—and why too much groupthink is a guaranteed innovation killer.

Chapter 13

SURVEYS

Why They're a Waste of Time

Another great saboteur of innovation is the overuse of surveys and focus groups.

Surveys are a particular problem for churches and nonprofits. These organizations typically operate like clubs or partnerships, wanting to hear from everyone before green-lighting anything that is significant or potentially controversial. So when leaders face a big decision, a survey typically is one of the first things suggested.

The business equivalent of a survey is a focus group. Like surveys, focus groups are an attempt to find out what people think in order to make wiser decisions. They have fallen out of favor in many business circles, which is a good thing, because in most cases, surveys and focus groups provide little useful information. More often than not, they're a colossal waste of time.

THE CURSE OF ANONYMITY

The biggest problem with surveys is that they are almost always anonymous. That alone renders most of them practically useless.

Not all opinions are equal. Opinions should be weighed, not counted. Some folks are chronic complainers, some never gripe, some are fools, and some people have the wisdom of Solomon.

Listening to a set of opinions without knowing who they come from is like flying an airplane into the clouds without knowing

105

which of your instruments are accurate and which ones are miscalibrated. You may get lucky and land the plane safely, but it won't be because of the input you received from the instrument panel. It will be in spite of the instrument panel.

Unofficial Surveys

Anonymity also rears its ugly head in unofficial surveys. These take place when members of a board or leadership team query their friends and acquaintances and then bring the results to a meeting.

They often present them this way: "I've talked to a lot of people and *they* think ..."

Interestingly enough, if the input from their friends and acquaintances is positive, they'll gladly reveal the names. But if it is critical or negative, they'll hesitate to reveal any names. They'll seek to protect the anonymity of their sources as if it's the only way to guarantee candor.

Don't let them get away with it.

If you want to make wise decisions, you can't allow any anonymous *theys* to have a place in your meetings. Once they've been given a voice, they become incredibly powerful. Most boards and leadership teams fear their wrath and assume they're representing hordes of other folks. Just a couple of theys can seem like hundreds.

The truth is that, once identified, *they* often turn out to be nothing more than a handful of people who everyone already knew opposed the idea. Their power disappears the moment they step out from behind the cloak of anonymity.

That's why at North Coast we have a strict and simple rule: no name, no input.

If someone says, "I've talked to a lot of people and *they* think ...," I always ask, "Who are *they*?"

If I'm told, "I'm not sure they would be comfortable if I used their names," I always say, "Then I'm not comfortable hearing what they have to say. I have no way to weigh it."

Self-Deceptive Surveys

You may be thinking, "Yes, but not all surveys are anonymous."

That's true. But even nonanonymous surveys have a serious built-in flaw.

When asked to self-report behavior, we tend to cast ourselves in the best possible light. It's human nature. We overstate the positive and understate the negative. We give ourselves the benefit of the doubt. So when people are asked in a survey (especially one with names attached), their answers usually have more to do with their good intentions than their real-life actions.

For instance, if you ask a group of church members how many of them would be willing to commit to a Bible reading program in order to read through the Bible in one year, lots of them would say yes. But when it comes time for them to actually sign up, the number will always be much less.

It's the same with regard to almost anything you can survey. Ask a group of people if they want to save for retirement, improve their marriage, or get out of debt. You'll get lots of wishful thinking and little reality. Many will say, "Yes, we want to do that." But few will open an IRA, head to a counselor, or cut up their credit cards.

COUNTING THE WRONG VOTES

Still another major problem with surveys is that most boards and leadership teams count the wrong votes. They count the "no" votes.

When it comes to innovation, the only votes that matter are the yes votes. You need enough yes votes to support a trial run. (Otherwise, it's time to step back and retool.) But once you have enough yes votes to give something a try, go for it. If it proves to be a truly great idea, the number of no votes won't matter. They'll change their votes and minds soon enough.

The problem with counting no votes is that none of us knows ahead of time how we will respond to something that does not yet exist. Surveys and focus groups are notorious for rejecting new innovations or changes because those surveyed concluded that something that didn't yet exist would be just like something that already existed.

Then they decided that the new concept, item, or program was a bad idea based on the comparison.

Consider the minivan. Before it was developed, market surveys showed virtually no interest in them. Nobody wanted a station wagon on a truck chassis. But that's not what a minivan was. That's just what they thought it was. Once they actually saw one, more than a few soccer moms decided they not only liked the concept; they had to have one.

I had the same experience when I first heard about the original iPad. I couldn't imagine why anyone would want a touchscreen tablet that was too big to be a phone (and didn't have telephony capabilities anyway) and was too underpowered to replace a laptop. I realized it might have a certain coolness factor, but at its high price point, I saw no value in it.

Nevertheless, one of our staff members waited in line to be among the first to own one. That afternoon, he brought it to the office. I went by to see it. I used it for about five minutes and then immediately went to my office, got online, and ordered the biggest and best model they had. I was bummed when I found out it was back-ordered. I wanted it right now. I needed it right now. Badly.

But had you asked me a week earlier in a marketing survey whether I would ever buy one, I would have given it two thumbs down.

That's why serial innovators don't bother taking surveys to gather opinions. They know that after the results are in, most people will count the no votes and give up on an idea. But when it comes to innovation, they know that the most important votes are the yes votes.

ASKING THE WRONG PEOPLE THE WRONG QUESTIONS

Another serious problem with surveys is that organizations often use them to ask the wrong people the wrong questions.

For instance, a number of years ago a national radio ministry took a survey in response to growing complaints about its ever-increasing emphasis on politics. The host felt the program was heading in the right direction. But ratings and donations were down. At the same time, the mailbag was mixed. The host and show were receiving an increasing number of complaints. But they were also receiving a growing number of letters and emails praising the direction of the show. So they decided to take a survey of current donors and listeners to decide what to do.

The results revealed little dissatisfaction. The respondents overwhelmingly approved of the increased political focus. The host felt vindicated and the show continued down the same path.

For a while, listenership and donations held steady. There was even a brief uptick after the survey. But it wasn't long until the downward slide resumed and donations and listenership continued to decrease.

What happened?

The radio show and host had made a classic mistake. They asked the wrong people the wrong question. Of course those who continued to donate and listen to the show liked the direction it was taking. That's why they gave money and why they tuned in. It didn't take a survey to figure that out.

What the radio host and show needed to know was why lots of other people had stopped giving and stopped listening. To find that out, they should have surveyed those who no longer donated and no longer tuned in. They were the ones who had the answers as to what it would take to stop the bleeding and bring the ratings back up. Their answers would have been markedly different from the answers of those who still donated and listened.

The same thing happens when a declining church decides to survey its congregation to figure out how to start growing again. The current attendees will almost always say, "Don't change anything, we like it just the way it is." But that's not very helpful if the church wants to know why people left or why visitors try it once and never come back again. They're asking the wrong people the wrong question.

Or consider the demise of old-school department stores. Most were way ahead of the game in terms of gathering and using sales information to carefully target their customers, especially their top customers. They were surveying them all the time. They knew exactly what they wanted, and they provided it for them.

But the old-school department stores failed to know their

lower-tier customers and people who weren't their customers. When Walmart, Target, and other big box value stores targeted these folks and a younger generation that wasn't yet wealthy enough to be top spenders, it wasn't long before they had them in their grasp. The department stores never knew what hit them. They were so busy focusing on their longtime big spenders that they lost out on everyone else, including an entire generation.

CONFUSING BUY-IN WITH PERMISSION

Finally, boards, committees, and leadership teams often turn to surveys because they confuse the need for buy-in with the need for permission. They think they need to get everyone aboard before successfully making major changes or trying anything new. So they survey the troops to see what they think in the hope of finding a path to broad acceptance.

This is a waste of time. Broad buy-in is almost impossible to get on the front end of any significant innovation or change. Remember, so-called mid-adopters won't buy into a new idea until they know who else is for it. Late adopters won't buy into it until everyone else is for it. Insisting on buy-in (or searching for it) is an exercise in futility.

Serial innovators and successful change agents don't seek buy-in. They seek permission. They know they can't get buy-in on the front end of something that is genuinely new or different. So they simply ask, "Can we try this?" They know that such permission is relatively easy to get, even when people think your idea is crazy or has no way of working. As long as they don't have to put their name on it or pay for it, most people will say, "Fine, go ahead."

Holding innovation and needed change hostage to the results of a survey inevitably sabotages the organizational health we're trying to foster. It falsely assumes that the way to the future is found on the path of least resistance. But in reality, it's a great way to ensure that nothing new ever gets off the ground.

Chapter 14

PAST SUCCESSES

How Yesterday's Success Sabotages Tomorrow's Innovation

Success can be dangerous. In the spiritual realm, it often leads to an arrogance that looks down on others and presumes that God is lucky to have us on his side. It's a grave error. It has led to many a shocking spiritual downfall.

But success can also be organizationally dangerous. Though it sure beats failure, it carries with it the same risk of arrogance and the same high odds of a shocking and unforeseen downfall.

It's always tempting to take too much credit. We'd like to think that our success is the result of working harder, smarter, and having more talent than everyone else. But in reality, success is usually the result of a confluence of factors. It's the result of hard work, wise decisions, and a generous portion of good luck, sometimes even blind luck.

We tend to forget or take for granted fortuitous timing and divine coincidences, and the important role that people and things completely out of our control played in our success. The view through the rearview mirror can be a bit fuzzy.

That's where arrogance creeps in. As soon as we think that our success was all of our own doing and that we could do it over again if given the opportunity, we stop listening. We no longer learn. We pontificate.

111

Why? Because we think we know it all.

And in one sense, we may be right.

We may know it all in terms of how to *become* successful.

But what we don't know (and often don't realize we don't know) is what it will take to remain successful. That's an entirely different set of information.

THE "NOT INVENTED HERE" SYNDROME

One of the most common forms of organizational arrogance is found in the rejection of anything "not invented here." It shows up as a lack of interest in fledgling technologies, methods, or programs that work elsewhere. It discounts and rejects the ideas, innovations, and successes of others. It turns an entire organization into a late adopter of anything that's not homegrown.

You'll often find this attitude in the long-established church that criticizes and resists the innovative approaches to ministry that newer or less established churches try. It writes them off, only to see them become mainstream in a few years, and misses the boat because of it.

It's what caused Atari and Hewlett-Packard to ridicule Steve Jobs' and Steve Wozniak's personal computer. According to Jobs, the interaction went something like this: "So we went to Atari and said, 'Hey, we've got this amazing thing, even built with some of your parts, and what do you think about funding us? Or we'll give it to you. We just want to do it. Pay our salary, we'll come work for you.' And they said, 'No.' So then we went to Hewlett-Packard, and they said, 'Hey, we don't need you. You haven't got through college yet.'"[11]

Very few sea-change innovations come from within mature and well-established organizations. They usually start with outliers who aren't even on the radar screen yet. A "not invented here" syndrome shuts out most of these innovations because only the homegrown variety gets a hearing. That's devastating to an organization's future.

From the top of the mountain called Success, these new ideas and duct-taped prototypes tend to look more like distractions than golden opportunities. That's why so many successful leaders and organizations ignore them. They figure they have more important things to do.

In reality, nothing could be farther from the truth.

One of the most important things a leader and leadership team must do is to look out the window. They need to see what's happening "out there," because out there is where the future lies, both in terms of unforeseen dangers and amazing opportunities.

But once a "not invented here" mindset takes over, no one bothers to look out the window anymore. They're too busy looking in the mirror and admiring what they see.

OVERVALUING EXPERIENCE

Another common problem that follows success is a tendency to overvalue experience.

Experience is a wonderful thing. It provides a wealth of knowledge that can be learned only over time. It brings perspective. It's a key component of wisdom. But experience (especially highly successful experience) can also produce an arrogance that discounts anything it doesn't fully understand or hasn't yet seen. And it's often particularly dismissive of anything proposed by the young and inexperienced, summarily writing them off as unworthy of a second look.

I've experienced this from both sides.

When I was in my midtwenties and early thirties, I espoused almost all of the same ideas and concepts that were later credited as being innovative and core to the growth and success of North Coast Church.

But when I shared them with older and more successful pastors (a rather large group at that time), not once did anyone delve deeper to see if there was any validity to what I was advocating. Not once.

Without fail they brushed me off, informing me that my ideas would never work and that I'd understand why once I had more experience under my belt.

Yet years later, some of these same leaders and churches now come from across the country to see and learn from what we were doing. They even take notes.

What changed?

Not much. The core ideas and ministry paradigms are still the same today as they were then. The only difference is that North Coast is now one of the larger churches in the country and I have gray hair. We have experience, so they listen.

But now the tables have turned. I'm the one with a wealth of experience. North Coast is the large and well-known church, and it's tempting for our leadership team to overvalue our experience and slough off the new ideas and insights that come from small and not yet "successful" leaders and churches.

But if we do that, we're doomed. Our past will be brighter than our future.

The fact is, most of the new paradigms, programs, and innovations that will be crucial to our success in the future are already being tried somewhere. Inexperienced leaders who aren't yet on the radar screen are putting them into practice and talking them up.

That's why it's so important for leaders of successful organizations to aggressively fight off the tendency to overvalue experience. The more of it we have, the more we tend to value it, and the harder it becomes to listen to those who have the answers we need but not the resume that impresses.

It's an age-old problem. Young leaders seem to get younger every year. But they aren't. They're the same age we were when we started out. They have great new ideas and insights that are already in early bloom. Some of them see the future with 20/20 vision. Someday they will be the sages. People will sit at their feet. Why not get a head start and listen to them today?

Ironically some of these future sages are right under our noses, but we've not yet noticed them because they've not yet worked their way up the food chain.

They're what I call young eagles. They can be found within almost every organization. But more often than not, their wings are clipped by leaders and leadership teams that overvalue experience and dismiss inexperience. They're forced to pay their dues, wait their turn, and keep their beaks shut.

If they want to fly, they have to go elsewhere.

Sadly, most of them do.

Worse, most leaders and organizations never even notice when they leave, because they never paid any attention when they were present.

TRUSTING THE RECIPE

Another common downside of success is a tendency to overtrust the recipe. When something works extraordinarily well, it's natural to assume that if it works here, it will work everywhere.

But our recipes for success are seldom as transferable as successful people and organizations think. There are too many contaminating variables, including an ever-changing cultural context.

When a thriving business in one part of the country decides to expand to another part of the country, odds are good that it will struggle. A great concept in Kansas City seldom comes off as being so great in Seattle.

When two successful companies merge, it can look good on paper. They wouldn't be doing it otherwise. Smart people sign off on the deal, convinced that two winners will make a champion. But in the real world, this rarely works as advertised. When highly successful corporate cultures combine, the normal result isn't synergy; it's conflict, because the successful recipe for one seldom works for the other.

Or consider what typically happens when a highly successful leader jumps from one industry to another. Sometimes it works out great. But often it's a disaster. Again, it's because the recipe for success in one field is seldom the recipe for success in another.

This reminds me of something I learned from a San Francisco baker. Like many tourists, I love the sourdough bread they bake and serve there. I always wondered why it tastes so much better and why no one has taken the recipe to other cities. It seemed like a no-brainer, a money-making idea to be sure.

Then I learned that the real secret to the San Francisco taste is not the recipe. It's a bacterium that thrives in the area. When the yeast ferments, its spores give the bread a distinctive taste. The San

Francisco bacterium is different from the spores that thrive in Dallas, LA, or New York. So even if you use the same recipe and starter, their bread won't taste like it was made in San Francisco. The taste is impossible to duplicate without the bacterial mix found in San Francisco's air.

I think that's a great way to think about success. It's not always found by following the recipe. It also matters where you do the cooking. There is no guarantee that what works well in one time and place will work in another. But that's a hard lesson to accept, once we've found a recipe that works.

Another variation of this error occurs when we assume that whatever worked in the past will work in the future. When we fall into the trap of overtrusting in yesterday's recipe based on yesterday's success, we will fail even to consider new innovations and paradigms because the things we did yesterday worked so well.

Consider Montgomery Ward, the once high-flying retailer. After adding a retail component to its dry-goods mail-order business, it rapidly became a retail powerhouse by buying up big city properties at rock bottom prices during the Depression.

When its competitors began moving out to the suburbs, the president of Montgomery Ward, Sewell Avery, refused to follow. He was convinced that another financial meltdown would come soon. So he hoarded cash, dug in his heels, and waited for another opportunity to buy up properties at deeply distressed prices.

But the next depression never came. The suburbs flourished. The inner cities died. His previously successful recipe failed miserably. And his company went out of business with barely a whimper in early 2001.

Now, before we come down too hard on poor Mr. Avery, we need to remember that we are not all that different. Once we find something that works, most of us have a hard time believing that it won't work everywhere and anytime.

For proof of this, just look at the long list of leaders and organizations (churches included) that once were great but missed out on the next wave because they failed to see it coming or were too busy doing what they'd always done.

IBM once received 70 percent of all money spent on computer purchases. GM once dominated 60 percent of the US auto market. Sony once controlled the market for personal portable music. CompuServe and Prodigy once battled for control of the internet. Lehman Brothers and Bear Sterns were investment giants, and they disappeared overnight. Most of the largest churches from fifty years ago have little influence today.

These weren't stupid people. They were simply blinded by their success. They overtrusted the recipe.

ADULATION

A final danger of success is that it creates an aura of invincibility and, with it, unwarranted adulation.

Adulation is a close cousin to arrogance and just as dangerous.

When arrogance strikes, we stop listening to our critics. When adulation strikes, we no longer have critics. Both will mess you up. Big time.

Adulation tends to silence the hard questions that need to be asked. When everyone around you assumes that you are right, no one wants to be the jerk who foolishly challenges the expert. No one wants to risk saying something stupid. So even if they have doubts, most people will keep their doubts to themselves.

When that happens, it's hard to lead well.

Pushback and hard questions are important parts of the innovation process. They derail our dumb ideas. They refine our great ideas. They turn good ideas into great ideas. Without pushback and hard questions, it's hard to know which is which.

I've found that a long string of successes will cause most people to downplay or forget about our mistakes and failures. It's human nature. Lots of people want gurus who are always right and organizations that never fail.

They don't exist.

But we wish they did.

· ◉ ·

SABOTAGING INNOVATION

Success is a great thing. It's what we're all aiming for. But it has its dangers. They remind me of a principle from mountain climbing: the closer you get to the top, the greater the danger you're surrounded by.

Every mountain climber would rather be approaching the peak than stuck back at base camp. Every leader would rather have success than failure or mediocrity. But only a fool forgets that the higher you go in mountain climbing or leadership, the greater the risk to your future. It's not a time for cockiness. It's a time for gratitude and caution. It's a time to listen to those you might be tempted to write off.

Part Five

BREAKOUT DECISIONS

Chapter 15

WHEN YOU'VE HIT THE WALL

Breaking Through Barriers of Competency and Complexity

Sooner or later, every leader hits the wall. Every organization and leadership team runs up against barriers that they cannot seem to overcome. What used to work well no longer works so well — or it no longer works at all.

Not many see it coming. It's usually a surprise, even if it shouldn't be. Sometimes it's the result of a long and slow process that no one noticed, like a "sudden" flat tire caused by overworn tread. Sometimes it really does come out of nowhere, without warning, bringing everything to a screeching halt.

Leaders and organizations respond to hitting the wall in different ways. I liken their various responses to someone who walks up to a lunchroom vending machine that they've used every day, puts their money in, makes a selection, and finds that nothing comes out.

Some leaders respond by putting more money into the machine. They're convinced that if they just keep doing what they've always done, the machine will somehow start working again.

Others go looking for help. They jump from consultant to consultant, conference to conference in the hope that someone will come and fix the machine for them.

Some start shaking the vending machine. They make lots of tweaks in an effort to shake something loose and get things working again.

Some focus on the mechanical problems. They double-check that the unresponsive machine is still plugged in. Leaders like this tighten up protocol and procedures, pulling out the employee manual to make sure everyone is doing what they are supposed to.

Finally, some leaders are like the guy who checks to see that no one is watching and then gives the vending machine a swift and vicious kick (as if that will teach it a lesson). They have a meltdown. They scream and shout at everyone as if that will fix the problem.

It's one thing to pay for a soda and not get what you ordered. It's another to be leading an organization that suddenly stops responding. When you do the same things you've always done but no longer get the same results, it's not only frustrating; it's scary. Most leaders and organizations have no idea what has happened, much less what they should do next.

Hitting this wall can usually be traced back to one of three things: (1) we've outgrown our leadership skills, (2) our organization has outgrown its structures, or (3) we've been blindsided by a cultural shift we never saw coming.

The first step in breaking through is to figure out which one it is.

LEADERSHIP SKILLS

Every leader has a ceiling. It doesn't matter how much training, commitment, or hard work we put in, we can't exceed that ceiling.

This doesn't mean that what *appears* to be a leader's ceiling is always his or her actual ceiling. Training and hard work can push us beyond what we thought we were capable of doing. But eventually, we'll reach our real ceiling. And when we do, nothing can take us beyond it.

I remember one staff member who consistently hit the wall anytime anything he led approached 100 to 125 people. That was his ceiling. His teaching gifts, relational bandwidth, and administrative skills wouldn't let him go beyond that.

I think of another person who gave me wise advice until we reached a few thousand people. But once we passed that number, most of his advice was far less valuable. His instincts constantly steered him (and me) toward a lid of two or three thousand people.

Those are genuine leadership ceilings. There is nothing that can be done to take these leaders beyond their ceiling. It's who they are. It's in their leadership DNA.

So what do you do if your church or organization hits the wall because of your leadership ceiling? What do you do if you have a staff member who hits the ceiling?

Does that mean *you* have to go?

Does it mean *they* have to go?

Not necessarily. I'd argue that far too often when an organization hits the wall, the leader falls on his sword or heads out of town, the assumption being that someone else will come in and take it to the next level. But more often than not, that next level is down a notch or two.

Hitting the wall is not always a bad thing. It might mean that your church or organization is in trouble. But it also might mean that you've become all that you're supposed to be.

Let me explain.

Addicted to Growth

Lots of leaders and organizations become addicted to growth. It's a particular problem for highly successful leaders and organizations. For years, everything heads up and to the right. Everyone assumes that this is the order of things, the predictable result of good and wise leadership.

This sets them up to believe a dangerous lie: that healthy things always grow and multiply.

Believing this lie gives successful leaders permission to look down on those who don't grow as fast or large. But such thinking is a disaster waiting to happen. It sets up leaders and organizations for needless angst. It eventually leads to panicked leadership transitions. It often ends up destroying everything the leadership of the organization has previously accomplished.

The fact is, nothing grows and multiplies forever. The idea that healthy things do is a silly myth.

Those who buy into the myth of endless multiplication and growth think that it's an idea supported by God's creation. But it isn't. There is nothing in the biological world that supports the idea that healthy things endlessly multiply and grow. In fact, the created order teaches quite the opposite. Only the lowest forms of life continually multiply and grow during their entire lifetime. The higher you move up the food chain, the shorter the period of multiplication and growth.

The popular idea that healthy churches and businesses will multiply and grow forever is hogwash. Healthy, living things grow to a size determined by their DNA and environment. Some grow to become ants, some elephants. But once they reach their predetermined size, they spend all their energy sustaining what they've become. They don't keep growing larger.

The only way they grow beyond their predetermined size is with steroids.

Sadly, many leaders turn to organizational steroids when their growth slows or stops. They panic and chase after the latest gimmicks and programs in the mistaken belief that bigger is always better. They churn and burn staff in an endless search for someone who can take them to the next level.

But if it's a level they're not programed to reach, they'll never get there. And if they aren't careful, they'll lose what they were designed to become in the mad pursuit of becoming something they were never meant to be.

Like all addictions, the addiction to growth can bring a short-term high. The uptick that organizational steroids bring can be gratifying. But it's always at the cost of long-term health. It's simply not worth it.

Leadership as Art

It's not always easy to know whether you've hit a wall or simply need more training and tools. One reason is that leadership is an art. Not only do we have a ceiling; we also have a specific skill set. Not every artist works well with every medium. At the end of the day, a leader is much more of an artist than an engineer. And that means that there are some skills we will never be able to master.

Let me explain.

I can't sing. I have absolutely zero musical gifts. When I try to convey to my wife a tune or sing a song from the past, she looks at me like I'm an idiot. She has no idea what I'm trying to communicate.

If you offered me the best vocal coaching in the world, it wouldn't matter. I still couldn't sing. And a change in venue won't help either. I sound bad in the shower.

But give that same coaching and training to a gifted singer and it's likely to take them to the next level. Put them in the right venue and they'll shine.

That's how leadership coaching, training, and placement work. They can refine and even improve the skills that people already have. But they can't give skills to someone who lacks them in the first place. They can't push someone to a level beyond the potential within them.

When an organization hits the wall, it's legitimate for a leader to ask, "Am I the lid? Have we outgrown my leadership skills?"

If the answer is no, it's time for more training and coaching. Most of us can get better at what we're already good at.

But if the answer is yes, it doesn't mean it's time to move on. It may mean it's time to settle in and maintain what has been built. "Are we supposed to grow more or is this our built-in limit and DNA?" is a difficult question to answer. It demands serious deliberation. It should not be answered in a knee-jerk fashion.

ORGANIZATIONAL STRUCTURES

A second reason why organizations hit the wall is because they've outgrown their structures. The *way we do things* often puts a lid on the *things we can do*. No organization can outgrow the ceiling of its policies, procedures, and practices.

For instance, when our church was small, we had a policy of holding congregational meetings to make major decisions. We'd have a meeting and ask everyone to vote on the issue at hand. It worked well. It created buy-in and accountability.

But as we grew, that policy became a lid. To say it got unwieldy would be an understatement. Today, with well over nine thousand people showing up at our various weekend services, it would not only be unwieldy; it would be impossible. We'd have to rent a sports arena to pull it off.

Imagine if we had not been able to jettison that policy (and many others that were designed for a neighborhood church of a few hundred). Our growth would have hit an impenetrable wall. There's no way we could have moved beyond it. At best we would have capped out at a couple of thousand people each weekend.

Organizational structures are like gravity. They can be temporarily overcome with lots of ingenuity. But eventually they will win. They always do. That's why organizations always settle in at a size that perfectly matches their policies, procedures, and structures.

It's also why churches and businesses that hit the wall should ask, "What policies, procedures, and practices have put a lid on our potential?" And if they find any, they need to have the guts to change them or the honesty to admit that their policies, procedures, and structures are more important than their mission.

CULTURAL SHIFTS

A third reason why organizations hit the wall can be traced to unforeseen major cultural changes. Culture is always changing. But some changes are sea changes. When they take place, nothing works like it used to.

Let me share an illustration from the church world.

In the 1980s and '90s, excellence was a widely held cultural value. *In Search of Excellence* was a bestseller. Success and conspicuous consumption to prove you were a success were in. Everyone wanted to be a leader. As a pastor, you could guarantee a big crowd for any series titled "How to Be a Successful (fill in the blank)."

In this cultural environment, a number of savvy churches began to offer preaching, programing, music, and facilities marked by excellence. They ended up reaching a ton of dechurched boomers who had grown up in schlocky churches with second-class programs in third-class facilities.

Boomers were hip, the trendsetters of the day. Though they had bailed out of their churches, they hadn't written off Jesus, the Bible, and God. They flocked back when some churches began to offer a culturally relevant ministry, one that actually fit with the world they lived and worked in the rest of the week.

Now fast-forward twenty years. The culture has radically shifted.

Excellence is no longer a preeminent value; too much of it and you come off as slick, phony, or worse. In a world of high-def, companies and videographers spend millions to make commercials that look like they were shot in a garage with an old camcorder.

Conspicuous consumption to prove your level of success is not only out; it's embarrassing, sort of like an old guy in a speedo. Simple living is no longer something to be ashamed of; it's something to brag about.

The keys to reaching the current culture are no longer excellence and the trappings of success. That day has passed. There are two new keys: authenticity and compassion.

It doesn't matter whether you are a church or a business; everyone wants to know whether you're the real deal and whether your organization is doing something for others. It doesn't matter whether someone is seventeen or seventy. If you come off as either phony or selfish, they'll write you off.

Dramatic cultural changes like this can pull the rug out from under previously successful organizations. Those that confuse their previous cultural adaptations with timeless values are especially vulnerable. They can unwittingly turn a method into a core value and end up holding on to old methods and strategies long after the culture has abandoned them.

For instance, many of the churches that succeeded by using excellence as a tool to reach people eventually turned excellence into a core value. When the culture changed, they hit the wall. The very thing that used to draw large crowds of boomers suddenly repelled a younger generation. Their churches grew gray overnight.

So what did they do? They ramped up the quality a notch or two.

But their problem was not a lack of excellence; it was a lack of cultural connection. They still had a great product. They just no longer had the right packaging. Improving the old-style packaging just made things worse.

. ● .

It's not always easy to understand what happened when you hit the wall. It often seems to come out of nowhere. But the first step is to figure that out, because what you do next should always be determined by the facts of what just happened.

Have we hit a built-in ceiling of leadership?

Have we hit the built-in ceiling of our organizational DNA?

Have we hit a structural ceiling that can be busted through with structural changes?

Have we hit a ceiling of cultural disconnect?

It's important to carefully consider each of these questions. The answers to them will make your next steps obvious. As the adage says, "Once you get the facts, the answers will practically jump out at you."

BREAKING THROUGH

The Need for New Advisors

The typical response to hitting the wall is to work harder, work smarter, and do better. We focus on effort, efficiency, and quality. And often, that solves the problem. Redoubling our efforts in any one of these areas can have a huge impact. Improving all three usually takes us to new heights. That's why we tend to go there first. But what happens when greater effort, improved efficiency, and better quality don't fix the problem?

Assuming you've not reached your God-ordained ceiling and there are still heights to scale, one of three things must change — and in some cases, all three. You'll need (1) new advisors, (2) new expectations, and/or (3) new structures.

I liken the need to make these changes to fixing the crimp in the hose that always happens when I try to wash my car. Once the hose gets stuck under a tire, it doesn't matter how much I turn up the flow of water. It doesn't matter what kind of special high-pressure nozzle I put on the hose. The amount of water coming out of the end of the hose won't exceed the amount that the crimp point lets through. And the only way to fix it is to go to source of the problem. I need to pull the hose out from under the tire.

In much the same way, our leadership pipeline can become crimped. Shortsighted advisors, unrealistic expectations, and crippling structures can severely limit what comes out of our organizations and leadership.

The only way to release the flow again is to go to the source of the problem and make some changes. Unfortunately, people and organizations aren't exactly like the tires on my car. They don't like to let go of the hose.

In fact, sometimes they prefer a trickle to letting everything flow freely. That's why they squeeze so tightly. That's why some hold on with a death grip. It can be quite a struggle to get the hose out of their hands. But it's got to be done; otherwise everything will come to a screeching halt.

NEW ADVISORS

Once we've hit the wall and can't break through with the usual strategies (effort, efficiency, and improved quality), the first thing most of us need to find is a set of new advisors.

But finding them, learning from them, and applying the things they can teach us is not as easy as it sounds. That's because most leaders and organizations resist outside advice. They assume that the answers to their toughest problems lie within those who know their field best. So they blow off the solutions of outsiders, convinced that they don't understand the real issues and the nuances of what they're facing.

But the answers to our most perplexing and difficult problems will seldom be found within. They'll almost always be found outside, often far outside among the outliers who see the world differently than we see it, unbound by our restricting assumptions and paradigms.

HOW MOST PROBLEMS ARE SOLVED

Most leaders and leadership teams do a good job of solving most problems. That's why we have success. We tend to follow a pattern that I call Me, My Team, My Tribe. It works like this.

When faced with a problem or roadblock, we turn within to find a solution. We think through, pray through, or work through the issue until a solution comes to mind. Then we apply it and move on. It's what makes a leader a leader.

If that doesn't work, we move from Me to My Team. We turn to coworkers and friends whose wisdom we trust. It's here that many innovative solutions are birthed, critiqued, and launched. Iron sharpens iron. Lessons are learned and experience gained. Over time, the collective wisdom of the team grows, enabling us to solve ever greater problems and issues. The whole becomes greater than the sum of its parts.

But eventually, the wisdom of the team runs out. We try everything we can think of and nothing works. We've hit a wall. So we turn to My Tribe.

My tribe consists of those who are outside of my specific organization, but with whom I have a natural affinity. Everyone (and every organization) has a tribe. When someone tells me they aren't part of a tribe, I simply ask who they read, what conferences they go to, who they look up to. Their answers tell me their tribe.

For a church, it's often the denomination or other churches of a similar persuasion. It's whom they hang with. For a business, it's usually those in the same industry. These are the people who speak our language. They deal with the same issues, share the same goals, and understand the challenges and subtleties we're facing.

The tribe often knows much more than the members of any particular team. That's why networking, peer-group learning, and conferences are so valuable. Whenever our tribe gets together, we tend to learn things we never would have figured out on our own.

Frankly, most of the issues an organization faces can be solved with the insights of Me, My Team, My Tribe. Many will go years without running into something that stumps the big three. But eventually it will happen. There will be an issue, a problem, or a roadblock that the leader, the team, and the tribe have no clue how to handle.

In many cases, that will be the end of the story. Because, sadly, lots of leaders assume that if they, their team, and their tribe have no answer, there is no answer. They settle in, assuming they've gone as far as they can go.

But there is one more place they need to check before settling in, convinced that there is no solution to the problem and no way to break through the wall. It's a place where the answers to a leader's and an organization's most difficult questions usually lie. It's outside the tribe.

OUTSIDE THE TRIBE

Many leaders never venture outside their tribe. Sometimes it's because of arrogance. They think they and their tribe have all the answers. Sometimes it's because of insecurity; they fear leaving their comfort zones. Sometimes it's because their tribe won't let them.

But if you want to break through your toughest barriers, you'll eventually have to go outside your tribe. That's where the answers have already been found and put into practice by other people and tribes who are unfettered by the paradigms, rules, and conventional wisdom that hold your tribe back. They have a different knowledge base, which allows them to see things from a different perspective.

I find it interesting that despite all the detailed instructions that God gave to Moses, the solution to organizing the Israelites came from his father-in-law, a man who didn't even acknowledge God until the night before he showed Moses how to avoid burnout and set up a system to administer justice and govern God's people.[12]

Many of us would have told Jethro to take a hike.

Moses told him, "Thanks, I needed that."

Or consider the lessons that a Formula One racing team taught a group of medical doctors. After completing a twelve-hour emergency transplant, the head doctor at Great Ormond Street Hospital in London watched a Formula One race. As a car pulled into the pit, he noted that the crew changed the tires, filled it with fuel, cleared the air intakes, and sent it off in seven seconds.

It struck him that it often took thirty minutes to untangle and unplug all the wires and tubes to transfer a patient from surgery to ICU. He wondered if a racing team could teach a hospital how to run an emergency room.

Imagine the pushback from the trained medical staff when the McLaren and Ferrari racing teams showed up to observe and advise them on how to improve their emergency services.

After all, what did they know about surgery?

Nothing.

What did they know about patient care?

Nothing.

What did they know about the complex interactions between doctors and nurses in an emergency room situation?

Nothing.

What did they know about speeding up complex processes?

Everything.

The result was a major restructuring of the process of handing over patients from surgery to intensive care. The Formula One teams suggested better training and actual rehearsals of the new protocols. They provided a step-by-step checklist covering each stage of the handover, including a diagram of the patient surrounded by the staff so that everyone knew their exact physical position as well as their precise task. They designated a leader (the anesthetist) who had authority to guide the team through the patient handover.

It almost halved handover errors.

The biggest problem the hospital faced (considered unsolvable and accepted as just the way things were) was solved by a group of people who knew nothing about the practice of medicine, emergency room procedures, or medical equipment. Unbound by the medical establishment's lens of experience, traditions, and conventional wisdom, they easily saw what the hospital tribe had missed.[13]

One of the great ironies of getting advice from outside your tribe is that it will make you look like an innovative genius within your own tribe. Many of the most innovative things done in one industry are nothing more than the application of common knowledge from another industry.

Some of the most creative and innovative things we've done at North Coast were simple rip-offs of things that other tribes considered no big deal. We have solved some of our biggest problems and launched our most significant innovations with lessons learned from In-N-Out Burger, Downtown Disney, stodgy CPA firms, Harley-Davidson, and educational theorists.

When they look at what we've done, they think, "What's the big deal?"

But when other churches look at what we've done, they often say, "Wow! How'd you think of that?"

YOU'LL NEED A PLAN

To take full advantage of the knowledge outside your tribe, you'll need a plan.

Without a plan, it will be hard to venture outside the safety of your own organization and tribe. The complexities of a growing (or even a stalled) organization consume massive amounts of time. Most leaders and leadership teams have little margin. Without a *plan* to look outside, they never have enough *time* to look outside.

I've known leaders who join diverse business groups or attend conferences that have little to nothing to do with their specific industry in order to expose themselves to the knowledge bases outside their tribe.

I've known leaders who have used travel, hobbies, classes, seminars, and online training to break out of their box.

I've long used a potpourri of reading sources from other fields to get me outside my tribe.

You'll have to figure out what works for you and your team. But I can assure you that you'll never learn the things that other tribes already know until you have a plan to visit them and learn.

YOU'LL NEED PERMISSION

You'll also need one other thing. You'll need permission.

Some organizations fear anything that comes from outside their tribe. If that's the case in your organization, you'll need to get permission ahead of time or else they'll reject everything you bring back from the outside.

If you're in ministry, step back and identify which key leaders and power brokers in your church naturally resist anything that comes from outside the tribe. Spend time with them to figure out how best to help them see that all truth is God's truth (even if it comes from somebody whose theology doesn't line up with yours point by point).

Otherwise, any ideas you bring from outside your tribe will be dead on arrival.

I learned this the hard way.

When I first brought to our leadership team lessons and insights from the business world, they fell on deaf ears. Some folks wanted a Bible verse for everything. They rejected powerful answers not on their merits but on their pedigree. They said things like, "The church is not a business."

I agreed. The church is not a business. But the moment we outgrew the home we started in, we were an organization. And businesses know an awful lot about organization and systems, much of which churches need to learn.

Frankly, I know the Bible well. But I've yet to find the verses that deal with hiring practices, parking problems, administrative workflow, or negotiating a lease. Maybe I just missed them. I don't know.

But churches aren't the only organizations that are slow to grant permission to learn from outsiders. I see this same reaction with some of the business leaders I do consulting for. When they bring back to their team the idea of inviting me to talk or meet with them, the initial reaction is often, "What can this guy know about our business? He's a pastor."

It's not that they're afraid that I'm going to take an offering or have an altar call. It's that they are just as closed-minded as everyone else. We all tend to think our tribe already knows everything important—or at least everything important to what we do.

• ● •

Fortunately, most leadership teams have what it takes to solve most problems. Between Me, My Team, and My Tribe there is an abundance of wisdom. But sooner or later, that well runs dry.

What we do next often determines how far we will go as leaders and organizations. Those of us who are humble enough to seek out new advisors usually find the answers we need, while those who are too arrogant to listen to outsiders usually end up complaining that there are no answers to be found.

Chapter 17

CHANGING THE RULES

Removing Unrealistic Expectations

One of the first things new advisors are likely to ask is, "Why are you doing *that*?"

Unencumbered by our long-held traditions, expectations, and standard operating procedures, they can see the unintended consequences of the patterns and behaviors we take for granted. They'll often suggest some major changes, especially in two areas: relational expectations and organizational structures.

In this chapter, we'll look at relational expectations. We'll see how unrealistic expectations can cause an organization to hit the wall and what it takes to change the relational rules of the game (both written and unwritten). Then in the next chapter, we'll look at organizational structures and what it takes to recognize and change the structures that hold us back.

Spoiler alert. Changing the relational rules of the game can be a bit scary. For some folks, it's terrifying. But if you've hit a wall of unrealistic relational expectations, changing the relational rules of the game and working through the fallout is the only way to break through to the next level. Sometimes you simply have to change the rules or lose.

EXPECTATIONS

Everyone has expectations. Sometimes they're realistic. Sometimes they're not.

When leaders have unrealistic expectations of staff, congregants, or customers, it creates frustration, conflict, and turnover. But when staff, board members, congregants, and customers have unrealistic expectations of a leader or leadership team, it can also create a mess, especially when those unrealistic expectations are relational.

For instance, in a startup company, the founder is generally available to anyone on staff. As the company grows, it soon becomes necessary to bring in additional upper management. But early staff members may resent this change to a more executive style of leadership and the loss of immediate and direct access. Some lose motivation. Some badmouth the changes. Some leave for a competitor.

But the entrepreneurial leader has no choice. Adding new management positions and changing relational patterns has to be done or the company will stall in its tracks. Without these changes, it can't move forward.

The same thing happens when a small church grows.

In a small church, people rightfully expect nearly instant access to their pastor. They expect to be known by name, to be counseled, married, and buried by whoever speaks on Sunday. It's the relational paradigm of a small church.

But as a church grows larger, it becomes nearly impossible for a pastor to meet those same expectations. It's no longer realistic for him to know every name and to counsel, marry, and bury everybody connected to the church. If he tries, he'll soon be the one needing counseling.

In one sense, everybody gets that. They know that the pastor of a growing church can't possibly meet every need. Most members of a growing congregation are good with that.

As long as he meets *their* needs, performs *their* wedding, and counsels them through *their* crisis, they'll be more than happy. It reminds me of something a mentor once told me. "Larry," he said, "everyone will tell you to slow down, but nobody really means it, especially if it impacts your relationship with them."

LOW-LEVEL FRUSTRATION

I always tell young leaders that you can't lead if you can't live with low-level frustration. Most of them think that I'm referring to the internal frustrations of leadership.

I'm not.

I'm referring to the low-level frustration that the people we lead will often feel toward us and our leadership team. A major part of successful leadership is seeing what needs to be done, finding a way to get it done, and nudging mildly resistant to strongly resistant people to go places they need to go, but don't want to go.

The fact is few people will understand why you do what you do. But that's why you're the leader and they're not. If everyone understood and agreed with everything their leaders did, there would be no need for leaders.

In the relational realm this is particularly true.

No one in your organization will ever consider their own expectations to be unreasonable. Few will be happy when you have to change the rules of access, especially if it locks them out of the decision-making process or insider knowledge and status. But if you grow, sooner or later, it will have to be done.

Jim Collins popularized the idea of getting the right people on the bus and then making sure we have the right people in the right seats. It has become a common metaphor for building a great staff and having a winning team.

He's right. We must have the right people in the right seats on the bus. But that's easier said than done. When it comes time to move someone to another seat, few will go willingly, unless of course we're moving them closer to the front of the bus.

Lots of leaders and teams get stymied because once they hit a wall of unrealistic relational expectations, they can't handle the pain and conflict that come with changing the rules. So they try to find a way to keep everyone happy, even if it means the wheels come off the bus.

138

WHERE THE PAIN COMES FROM

One of my greatest leadership mistakes was underestimating and devaluing the level of pain and loss that comes when the relational rules change. Like many leaders, I was personally willing to do whatever it took to fulfill the mission. For me, personal sacrifice and loss for the cause are a given. I don't begrudge them or resist them. They're simply the price of leadership.

I identify with the way the apostle Paul described his own approach to ministry: "I have become all things to all people so that by all possible means I might save some."[14]

But what I missed badly was that not everyone on our team or in our church was wired to be a leader. I made the mistake of assuming that everyone was just like me (or would be when they grew up). I figured they would handle the loss of power, prestige, or preference in the same way I did. Go home, kick the dog, and get over it.

I couldn't have been more wrong. Looking back, I was an idiot. And at one point, it cost me dearly. It even led to an attempted coup.

THE LOSS OF POWER

Whenever it's time to change the decision-making or reporting structures within an organization, someone loses power. It can't be helped.

As healthy organizations grow, they make room at the top. The number of people sitting at the leadership table grows. That adds new blood and new ideas. It keeps the young eagles around. It's how growing organizations stay fresh and innovative.

But sooner or later the leadership table gets too crowded. Communication suffers, meetings run too long, low-level conflict increases, and nothing much gets done anymore.

That usually means it's time to shrink the leadership table back to an appropriate size. But therein lies a problem. Who should stay at the new and smaller table, and who should go?

Having the right people at the new table almost always means that some folks who were there first will have to give up their seat. That's incredibly painful, even for those who know it's the right thing to do. It's excruciatingly painful for those who don't understand why they're the ones who no longer have a chair.

As a leader, it's vital to understand and acknowledge their pain. Go toward the problem. Ignoring it or hoping that it will go away won't work. It will only make the pain worse.

That doesn't mean that those who have lost power will suddenly agree or understand the changes. They seldom will. But it will do wonders for making sure that their pain doesn't turn into a festering wound that also hurts others.

Refusing to shrink the table or to put the right people in the right seats is not an option. Once you've hit a wall, you have to address who is at the table or you'll be stuck in neutral. Having people in power who shouldn't be in power is a guaranteed way to make sure that you remain stuck. You'll never break through the wall. That's probably what caused you to hit the wall in the first place.

THE LOSS OF PRESTIGE

Recalibrating relational expectations not only impacts who has power; it also impacts how people feel about themselves. It has been said that knowledge is power. That's true. But it's also prestige. That's why we gossip or tell stories that we were supposed to keep confidential. There's something about being in the know that makes us feel important.

Whenever someone on your team used to be in the know, but now no longer is in the know, expect them to experience a deep sense of loss and some occasional embarrassment.

Let me explain.

When it came time for our board to change its role from overseeing day-to-day details to more of a high-level governance model, it meant that they would be in the dark on some things they used to know about. The church had grown so large and complex that having the board involved in every decision was slowing things to a crawl.

So we all agreed on a new set of board guidelines and expectations that narrowed their scope of hands-on oversight. For the most part things went fine. But there were a couple of board members who periodically fell back into micromanaging. At first, I couldn't understand why. They had agreed to the changes, but every now and then kept reverting to the old rules.

Then it hit me. Almost every time that they demanded more day-to-day details, it was immediately after a social setting in which they had been asked about a decision the staff had made, but which they had no knowledge of.

I realized that subconsciously they found it devaluing and embarrassing to be in the dark, especially when they used to know everything. So at the next meeting, they'd ask lots of questions.

And it's not just the loss of insider information that causes this loss of prestige. The loss of easy access to a leader will do the same thing. When someone who once dropped into your office at will finds out they now need an appointment, they're bound to feel a great loss. It can't be helped.

But once again, any loss like this has to be personally addressed. People who have lost a sense of prestige need to know that you understand how they feel. That won't take away their pain. But it might take away the fight-or-flight response that often follows deep hurt and pain.

The fact is, if given a choice, most people in an organization will choose to maintain comfortable patterns of relationship over fulfilling the mission. That's why people who are passed over for promotions, demoted, or moved to another seat on the bus so often leave the church, nonprofit, or business that previously meant so much to them. Their embarrassment and sense of loss are simply too painful to handle, no matter how important to the mission the changes might have been.

Unfortunately, despite the pain it causes, there's no way around the need to change relational expectations when you've outgrown the old patterns and have hit the wall. You have no choice. It's the leader and leadership team's job to make these tough calls.

THE LOSS OF PREFERENCE

A final area of loss that comes with significant changes in relational patterns has to do with personal preferences. Easy access to leadership and positions at the seat of power generally come with lots of input into how things are done.

When that input is lost, many people discover that things are no longer done according to their liking. They lose their personal preferences.

Just like a loss of power and prestige, the loss of personal preference is a painful deal. It's why so many former leaders (board members, pastors, staff members, company presidents, and business leaders) have to get out of town once their gig is up. They have a terribly hard time accepting the fact that they no longer have a say in how things are done. And worse, they discover that some things are done in ways they don't approve of. Their loss of personal preference in an organization they have long helped to shape and lead can be devastating. So much so that in some cases they end up sabotaging the direction of the new leadership.

· ● ·

Changing relational expectations is never easy. But letting long-time congregants, customers, staff members, or former leaders have their way is a recipe for stalling. In most cases, it was doing things their way that caused you to hit the wall in the first place. Allowing them to continue to have their way ensures that your church or business eventually shrinks to a size that perfectly fits the way everyone wants to relate to one another.

CHANGING TRADITIONS

Removing Unhealthy Structures

When we've hit the wall and all the traditional breakthrough methods (greater effort, efficiency, and improved quality) haven't worked, it's not only time to consider new advisors and new patterns of relationship; it's also time to consider whether our traditions and organizational structures might be the culprits.

The good news is that changing organizational structures is relatively easy, *unless* of course they are traditional structures.

The bad news is that most organizational polices, procedures, and structures become traditions rather quickly. When most people think of an organizational tradition, they think of something with a long history. But that's not always the case. Lots of traditions are merely the comfortable and expected way of doing things around here, even though we haven't been doing it very long.

Traditional structures not only have the power of inertia behind them; they have the power of emotion. People find comfort in their traditions (even their new ones). Changing them is almost always an uphill battle.

I learned that the hard way as a young pastor of a new church. The church was just a few years old and was meeting in a high-school cafeteria when I arrived. I figured since it was so new, it had no traditions.

I was wrong. Dead wrong. Every time I tried to change anything, someone would tell me, "That's not the way we do it around here."

I quickly learned that our church was like most organizations. The evolution of a deeply held tradition went something like this.

Year one: Why are we doing *that*?
Year two: Okay. Whatever.
Year three: But we've *always* done it this way.

That's what makes changing dysfunctional structures so difficult. After year three, they tend to have the power of tradition. But it matters not. They can't be left to run their course. Dysfunctional structures will run any organization into the proverbial wall. And if something isn't done to change them, the organization will inevitably shrink to a size that perfectly fits its policies, procedures, and structure.

IS IT WORTH THE BATTLE?

Not every goofy or annoying tradition and organizational structure is worth changing. Every organization has plenty of them. They seem to spontaneously generate. But a leader can't and shouldn't do battle with all of them. Every leader and leadership team has only a limited number of chips. Using them to change every policy, procedure, and practice that is merely annoying, ineffective, or a waste of time is seldom a good use of those chips.

That was the mistake I made in my early years of leadership. If something didn't help us accomplish our mission, I tried to kill it off. It nearly killed me off.

Since then I've learned that the important question is not, "Does this fail to help us fulfill our mission?" The important question is, "Does this *keep us* from fulfilling our mission?"

If something is a roadblock that keeps us from moving forward, it has to go. If it's merely an annoyance, it's probably best to put up with it until I have a ton of chips in the bank.

So what are the polices, procedures, and practices that have to go once you've hit the wall? Which ones are worth the battle? The

144

answer is that anything that (1) locks out fresh thinking, (2) derails the decision-making process, or (3) destroys flexibility has to go, the sooner the better. It's the only way you'll break through to the other side of the wall.

FRESH THINKING

I find that lots of organizations have polices and procedures that unintentionally lock out fresh thinking.

Because of the size of our church and my national network, I'm often asked whether I know of any potential candidates for an open staff position. My normal response is to ask for a copy of the job description and requirements. It always surprises me that most are filled with qualifications and requirements that have little to do with the job.

For instance, at the top of almost every list of job qualifications is a list of minimum educational and experience requirements. Right off the bat, that eliminates some great people. Ironically, a lot of the organizations that ask me for advice wouldn't have hired me for a job back when I was starting out. And their minimum qualifications for hiring would eliminate some of my best staff members, the very ones they'd like to hire away.

Shoot, Bill Gates, Steve Jobs, and Mark Zuckerberg wouldn't pass muster in the HR department of a lot of companies.

Any organization that automatically rewards experience and education unintentionally punishes inexperience and a lack of formal education. Over the long run, that will make it harder and harder for fresh thinking to have a voice. It will push young eagles to the bottom of the pile, keep fresh thinking at the back of the line, and pretty much guarantee that innovation happens elsewhere.

The rationale behind rewarding education and experience is a desire for safety, a preference for the known over the unknown. But when it comes to building an innovative and successful team, risk aversion usually turns out to be success aversion. Safe people are indeed safe, but they're seldom spectacularly successful.

Those who are most likely to bring genuinely fresh thinking to your organization are always a little bit weird. They are almost always too young, too inexperienced, or too idealistic to know that their ideas won't work. Which is exactly why you need them at the table.

Any policies, procedures, or traditions that lock them out are worth the battle to remove.

DECISION-MAKING

Another area where policies, procedures, and traditions can hold us back is in the decision-making process. When you've hit a wall, it's a good idea to ask if your decision-making process is structured to make bad decisions.

The most common problem is having too many people involved in the process.

The more people involved in the process, the more likely it is that most decisions will favor the status quo. As we saw in an earlier chapter, a gauntlet of committees will almost always derail innovation and fresh thinking, the desire for harmony gives veto power to the angry and stubborn, and groupthink leads to a politically correct rather than a brutally honest assessment. All of these contribute to organizational inertia.

Having too many people involved in the process also tends to slow everything to a crawl. Large groups seldom make quick and good decisions.

It takes nuanced thinking to make a good decision. But that bogs down most larger groups. And even when they try to work through the nuances of a tough decision, the key issues often will be boiled down to soundbites and simplistic solutions that can be easily grasped by everyone present.

In addition, the larger the group, the more likely it is that everything will need to be reviewed over and over. Someone will always have missed something (or the last meeting) and need to be brought back up to speed.

Finally, when polices and traditions involve too many people in the decision-making process, it's almost impossible to get everyone close enough to the facts so that they can make a wise decision.

Smart people make foolish decisions when they don't have accurate facts and firsthand knowledge of the key players. It forces them to rely on past experiences, hearsay, and assumptions.

I like to put it this way:

The Wisdom of Solomon + Inaccurate Information = A Fool's Decision

FLEXIBILITY

A lack of flexibility is another structural problem that's worth the battle. When policies, procedures, and organizational structures become too rigid, it becomes almost impossible to break through once you've hit the wall.

Flexibility is important because the only thing we can know for certain about the future is that it will be radically different from what we thought it would be. That's why it's so vital to build flexibility into the DNA of our organizational structures. Without it, it will be difficult to navigate the constantly changing landscape of the future.

For instance, consider the consequences of inflexibility as they relate to a budget. Inflexible budgets are horrible at handling opportunity because it just shows up. It never sends an email saying when it's coming. And unlike a crisis, which if it is serious enough will be taken care of, opportunity has to wait until it can be put in the budget.

But it doesn't wait. It just leaves. Which explains why organizations with rigid budgets usually have a long history of missed opportunities.

Another way of illustrating the advantage that flexible organizations have over rigid organizations can be seen in the fundamental differences between a blueprint and a game plan.

Blueprint organizations have a rule for everything. Once an architect finishes a blueprint, the contractor is expected to follow it exactly. He doesn't have the option of pushing a wall out a couple of feet or placing the plumbing on another wall. If he does, he'll be in big trouble with both the inspector and the architect.

Blueprint organizations also insist that everyone follow the manual exactly as it's written.

They also tend to live in the past. In fact, I've found that I can often tell with great accuracy what their big problems of the past were based on reading their current polices and procedures. It's as if they made a new lock every time another horse left the barn.

In contrast, game-plan organizations have a plan that is constantly adjusted as the game goes on. Game-plan organizations tell everyone to first try this, but then do whatever seems best if that doesn't work. A coach expects his players to make adjustments on the fly. It's part of what he coaches and trains them to do. His game plan has built-in options based on the score and time left in the game.

· ◉ ·

Hitting the wall is tough. It's no fun. But it can be a great opportunity for you and your organization, as well as innovation's best friend. That's because it's only when the old ways stop working that most people are willing to consider the new ways—the new advisors, expectations, and structures that will pave the way for tomorrow's adventure.

Part Six

WHY VISION MATTERS

Part Six

WHY VISION MATTERS

THE POLAROID PRINCIPLE

How Vision Works

Lots of people confuse mission with vision. Both are incredibly important. But while mission and vision are close cousins, they play different roles when it comes to innovation and leadership.

A mission statement explains why your church, nonprofit, or company exists. It clarifies what you're aiming at without much detail. It's a laserlike description of your ultimate goal. It describes the bull's-eye.

Vision is much more detailed. It's the narrative that describes what success is supposed to look like in detailed and real-life terms. It puts flesh on your missional bones.

If you have a clear mission statement but no corresponding detailed vision of what success looks like or how you plan to get there, the result will almost always be a confused and splintered team. Each member will seek to fulfill the mission in their own way, taking the path that seems best to them.

If you have a detailed vision without a clear mission statement, the result will almost always be lots of activity without any means of determining whether it's accomplishing anything. At the end of the day, there will be no way to measure success.

We've already seen in an earlier chapter the power of a clear mission statement to accelerate the innovation process. In this

151

chapter, we'll look at why clear and compelling vision is so important and how it's developed.

Unlike mission, vision often starts out fuzzy. It's a lot like an old-fashioned Polaroid picture; it becomes sharper and more focused over time. It can't be rushed. But if allowed to fully develop, it provides a clear and detailed description of what success looks like.

Once that happens, it becomes increasingly obvious which new ideas are merely novel and which ones have the potential to advance the cause. It makes many otherwise difficult leadership decisions a snap.

Vision also tends to expand over time. It becomes broader and more nuanced.

For instance, at North Coast Church, our mission is "Making Disciples in a Healthy Church Environment." Our original description of what that looked like included a vision of having at least 80 percent of our adult worship attendance meeting in a weekly small group. Later we expanded our vision with more details. We imagined our small groups taking the weekend sermon and digging deeper into the main topic. Still later we included a community-service component, casting a vision of each group taking on multiple service projects throughout the year.

This is just one example of the many areas where our vision has developed over time even though our mission has remained exactly the same.

So how does this thing called vision develop? What can we do to find, clarify, recalibrate, and communicate it in a way that makes a difference? Here are six things you'll want to keep in mind. They describe what it takes to move from mission to vision to reality.

1. YOU ALREADY HAVE A VISION

Sometimes leaders tell me they have no vision. But they're wrong. They always have a vision. It may be ill-defined, uncertain, or deeply buried. But it's there, even if only in nascent form. It always is.

Perhaps you've experienced something similar to the following conversation.

"Where do you want to go for lunch?"

"I don't care. Anywhere."

"How about McDonald's?"

"I guess I do care. Anywhere but there."

It's not until someone suggests a specific place, in this case McDonald's, that most of us realize that we actually do have a vision for lunch. It's not crystal clear. It's simply anywhere but McDonald's. But let someone suggest another place, perhaps Wendy's, and we realize it's even more specific: anything but fast food.

Getting in touch with our vision often starts with the extremes of what we dislike most and what we desire most. One of the easiest ways to uncover your vision is to ask yourself what are the things in your church, nonprofit, or company that you feel best about, and what are the things that cause you to feel most embarrassed or discouraged.

If you don't know where to start, start with what you don't want. It's often easier to get in touch with what we don't want than with what we want. Describe it in detail.

I've found that highly influential and innovative leaders almost always have a vision grounded in a unique combination of the worst and best experiences from their past. They dream of creating a place that proves that their bad experiences need not have happened, and a place where their best experiences are duplicated.

The most important thing about your vision is to make sure that it's an honest reflection of what you're passionate about and what you want to see take place. It has to be real. It can't be mere political correctness or a generic definition of success in your industry. Political correctness and marketing clichés aren't vision. They can't set you apart or get you in touch with your calling.

2. VISION EVOLVES

As we've already seen, vision evolves. It seldom pops out fully developed. It most often begins as a sense of direction. Then later, it becomes a specific plan. Finally, it ends up as a destination, though the final destination is often quite different from what we expected when the journey began.

Consider the famous expedition of Lewis and Clark. In many ways it's a perfect illustration of how vision evolves.

They started out with a crystal clear sense of direction. They were headed toward the Pacific Ocean in search of a northwest passage suitable for commerce. They laid out a plan to get there. But their plan changed almost daily in light of the shifting realities they experienced along the way. By the time they had reached their destination, the Pacific Ocean, they were no longer charting a river-based passage suitable for commerce. They'd already established that it didn't even exist. Instead, they were compiling a treasure trove of scientific and geographical discoveries that would pave the way for future exploration.

In the same way, successful and innovative leaders tend to start out with a destination in mind and head off toward it. But changing realities tend to mess up their plans. So they continually adjust, taking a slightly different route, refining their vision as they go along. At the end of the day, they present us with a gift called Oregon.

The fact is, most successful and innovative leaders don't control their destiny. They ride it out. They start with a vision and a goal and then follow it wherever it takes them. And it often takes them to places they didn't know existed when they started out.

3. VISION COMES FROM WITHIN

A compelling vision comes from within. When leaders develop their vision by looking out the window to see what everyone else is doing, they don't end up with a vision. They end up with a poor imitation of someone else's vision.

A God-given vision will always be unique, simply because every leader and every organization is unique. That's not to say you have to be radically different. It is to say that you have to be you.

To make sure your vision is aligned with your uniqueness as well as with that of your organization and the situation you find yourself in, it's helpful to ask a couple of questions.

The first question is, "Who is our leader?"

No vision can succeed without a strong alignment with the

gifts, skills, and passion of the directional leader. That's why vision almost always starts with the directional leader. It can and should be adjusted and fine-tuned by others, but if it starts elsewhere or fails to honestly align with the leader's gifts, skills, and passion, it has little chance of succeeding. It's a recipe for dysfunction, a short tenure, and an abundance of conflict.

The second question is, "Who are we?"

Just as no vision can succeed if it's misaligned with the leader, the same holds true for a leadership team. That's why it's important to honestly assess the gifts, skills, and passion of the team. They don't have to match the leader's exactly. In fact, most often, they shouldn't. But they need to be complementary. Their passion must flow in the same channel as the directional leader's or it won't be long until the leader, the leadership team, or the vision goes through some painful transitions.

4. VISION CLARIFIES PRIORITIES

Every organization has more opportunities than time, money, and energy to pursue them. That's where vision comes in. The clearer and more detailed our vision, the more obvious it will be which opportunities and new ideas ought to be pursued and which ones should be ignored.

This is one of the most important benefits of a clear and detailed vision.

Without a clear set of priorities, anything that brings in more people or money ends up looking like a great opportunity. But some things that bring in a temporary infusion of attendees, customers, or money aren't great opportunities. They're detours, undercutting and sabotaging our mission and vision.

For instance, a rush of customers you can't serve well will set you back. Those who have a bad experience will most likely be lost forever. It's certain that they will tell others about their negative experiences. Even if it puts some extra dollars in your pocket, in the long run, the results will be the same as if you had unintentionally purchased a batch of negative advertising.

I remember a friend who was a sucker for every new program that seemed to work elsewhere. He'd go to check it out and bring it back home. Though it often resulted in a temporary spike in attendance, it was always followed by a return to the previous norm. It never dawned on him that he was cannibalizing his vision or that the word on the street had become "I *used* to go there."

A clearly articulated vision keeps that from happening. It sets priorities that make it obvious when a so-called golden opportunity is in reality just a dangerous temptation.

5. VISION MATCHES REALITY

Leaders often assume that once they've figured out what they're supposed to do, they should do it immediately. But that's a big mistake. Wise leadership is not the art of the ideal. It's the art of the possible.

Imagine a general deciding that since the textbook battle plan always takes the high ground, he's going to storm the three hills surrounding the battleground, even though he has only enough soldiers and firepower to take two of them.

We'd consider him a fool. Dividing his troops and attacking all three hills at once would leave him with no hills conquered, lots of dead soldiers, and a reputation for snatching defeat out of the jaws of victory.

Yet that's exactly what many leaders and leadership teams do. They pursue the ideal no matter what the reality is. Once they see a hill that needs to be taken, they charge off to take it, even if they don't yet have the resources to win the battle.

Successful leaders and leadership teams don't go off half-cocked. They are realists. They're brutally honest with themselves. They don't try to do what they can't do. They know their strengths and weaknesses. They start with the low-hanging fruit they can reach before searching for a ladder to pick the tough stuff that's far out of reach.

They also tend to move forward at a steady but unrushed pace. They are more like a glacier than an avalanche. They embody the adage that we all tend to greatly overestimate what we can do in one year, and greatly underestimate what we can do in five.

An avalanche looks impressive. It's powerful, pushing lots of stuff down the hill. It knocks over and buries anything in its way. But come back a few years later and you'll be hard pressed to find any evidence that it did anything.

A glacier doesn't look like it's doing much. But it is. It's moving slowly and powerfully in one direction. Nothing stops it. And thousands of years later, it has carved out a Yosemite.

6. VISION SELDOM COMES OUT OF A COMMITTEE MEETING

As we saw in an earlier chapter, groupthink is one of innovation's worst enemies. It's also one of vision's worst enemies.

A realistic vision has to align with the passions, skills, and strengths of the leadership team and those who operate the organization. But it also almost always has to flow out of the heart of the leader. It seldom (if ever) comes out of a committee meeting.

There are many ways to design a house. But someone has to take on the role of head architect. You can't take a vote on each room. If you do, you'll end up with something resembling the Winchester House.[15]

That's not to say that the best and most innovative leaders act in isolation. It's simply to say that they don't take a poll or a vote when developing their vision. They typically work with a very small and tight-knit group.

Think of the way Steve Jobs, Jonathan Ive, and Tim Cook worked together at Apple. Jobs was the unquestioned leader. He didn't take straw polls or turn to focus groups. He looked within, designing products that he personally wanted to use. But he did listen carefully to both Ive and Cook, often adjusting his vision to what they saw and suggested. The result was some of the most groundbreaking and innovative products of the day.

Over the years, I've found that the best visionaries and innovators in nearly every field lead and innovate in much the same way. Whether they are leading a church, a nonprofit, or a company, they seldom act alone. And they often have a cord of three.

But they never have a committee.

Chapter 20

CREATING AND SUSTAINING VISION

The Leader's Role

Vision is fragile. It needs help—lots of help.

It can't spawn itself. It can't sustain itself. It can't recalibrate itself. It tends to leak and fade. If left to itself, it takes the path of least resistance. That's why someone has to continuously make sure that it remains appropriate, doable, and properly aligned with reality or it will morph into wishful thinking.

That's where a leader steps in. Ultimately vision is the leader's responsibility. It can't be delegated. It can't be neglected. It can't be presumed upon. It has to be monitored. And in particular, there are four things that demand a leader's attention. Here's a careful look at each one.

1. *VERIFY* THE VISION

A leader's first and foremost role is to verify the vision. That includes creating it (as we saw in the last chapter), but it also incudes monitoring it to make sure that it remains appropriate and doable. It's a leader's job to ensure that the hard questions are regularly asked and that the vision is constantly readjusted in light of the answers, even if the answers are uncomfortable or disappointing to hear.

Is This Appropriate?

A leader has to make sure that methods used to achieve the vision remain appropriate. Not everything that works is appropriate or ethical.

In the context of the church, a leader has to ask, "Does this align with biblical principles?" That doesn't mean everything has to have a Bible verse to support it. But it does mean we can't do anything that the Bible forbids or frowns upon.

In a business setting, the question is, "Is this ethical?" Merely legal is not the standard. Lots of things are legal but not appropriate. Perhaps the best way to shed light on the difference is to ask yourself this question: "What if what we are doing shows up on the front page of the newspaper?"

If your initial response would be, "Oh no!" then don't do it. It's not appropriate, no matter how common or legal it might be.

Is This Doable?

The second thing a leader needs to constantly verify is the likelihood of success. Is this still doable?

Again, as we saw in the last chapter, our vision has to be realistic or it's a pathway to defeat and disaster. But it's not enough only to ask that question at the beginning. We need to ask it continually. Some things that are realistic one day become impossible the next day. It's the leader's job to constantly check the reality gauge.

2. *COMMUNICATE* THE VISION

A leader also has the responsibility to communicate the vision. And the first step is to make sure that it's understandable.

That sounds obvious. But it's not. Lots of leaders communicate their vision in a way that confuses as much as it clarifies. To ensure that your vision is widely understood, it must be communicated in a way that is brief and eliminates all jargon and clichés.

Keep It Brief

Brevity is important. Just as with your mission statement, your detailed vision of what success will ultimately look like needs to be succinct enough that people can remember it and pass it on. It's not limited to a simple soundbite like your mission statement is. But it still needs to err on the side of brevity.

When I was working on my doctoral dissertation, my advisor gave me some advice that not only helped me clarify my dissertation project; it also helped me clarify my vision for North Coast.

He told me I wasn't ready to begin my research until I had it boiled down to an "elevator speech." He claimed that if I couldn't explain what it was about while traveling between the first and third floors, I didn't understand it well enough to get started.

He was right. I've found that if I can't explain a complex concept in a crisp way, it usually means that I don't understand it. That doesn't mean that the short version incorporates everything important. Of course it doesn't. But it does mean that I get the big picture and I've got my arms around the core of the idea.

It reminds me of the way Jesus answered a theologian who asked him which of the thousands of commands in Jewish scripture was most important. Jesus told him, "'Love the Lord your God with all your heart and with all your soul and with all your mind.' This is the first and greatest commandment. And the second is like it: 'Love your neighbor as yourself.' All the Law and the Prophets hang on these two commandments."[16]

His answer certainly didn't explain all the nuances of Scripture. But it explained everything that an illiterate farmer, maidservant, or shopkeeper needed to know to start living out his vision for their lives.

Avoid Jargon

It's also important to avoid jargon. It never helps. It only obscures your vision.

The problem is that we don't always recognize jargon as jargon. We use it because it conveys complex concepts in just a few words. Every field and industry has its own set of terms and phrases that are used as shorthand to convey complex and complicated concepts quickly. To insiders they are genuinely helpful.

But they are meaningless and confusing to those who haven't

yet been fully initiated. If you use any jargon, those who are new to your organization won't have a clue what you're talking about. But they won't tell you so. They'll act like they get it, because few of us are willing to ask for help when everyone else around us seems to understand what's being said. Instead we smile and fake it.

I remember asking a church-planter what his vision was for his new ministry. He told me that his dream was to become a church with "gospel-centered preaching that produces missional communities carrying out the Great Commission and the Great Commandment."

Ironically, his goal was to reach lots of non-Christians. Unfortunately, those non-Christians had no idea what he was talking about. The only people who understood what he meant where those who were already firmly entrenched within his tribe. Everyone else was left to feel stupid. His jargon turned an otherwise precise vision into something murky and obtuse.

Avoid Clichés

Clichés are similar to jargon but different. It's not that people won't understand them. It's that they're so generic and obvious that people won't care.

For instance, if someone tells me the vision for his company is to offer customers quality, reliable service with a friendly and knowledgeable staff, I've tuned out long before he's finished.

He doesn't have a vision. He has a series of clichés. There is nothing that stands out as unique or special. There's no track to run on. Who doesn't want to offer their customers quality, reliability, and service? Who doesn't want a staff that's friendly and knowledgeable? I've never heard of someone who dreamed of building a company offering junk, inconsistency, and poor service by a staff of rude and ignorant slobs.

Repeat It Ad Nauseam

The final step in communicating your vision is to repeat it ad nauseam.

Again, as with your mission statement, your detailed vision of what success looks like can't be repeated too often. Don't worry if people look bored. Don't worry if everyone has heard it a million times. Keep repeating the vision.

There will always be new staff members, congregants, and customers who don't get it yet. They are your primary audience, not the folks who've been around forever and roll their eyes when you repeat yourself once again.

In fact, I've noticed that those who are best at communicating the vision are often lovingly mocked (to their faces and behind their backs) for saying the same things over and over. But they don't care. They understand that the vision hasn't been fully communicated until *everyone* can describe it in detail without prompting. They understand familiarity isn't knowledge. They know it's a good thing when folks know the vision so well they can jokingly mimic the stump speech.

They've won.

They've communicated.

3. *BUILD A TEAM* AROUND THE VISION

The third responsibility of a leader is to build a team around the vision. That means putting an emphasis on those positions that are most crucial to the vision and making sure you've put the right kind of people into those slots.

For instance, since our vision at North Coast emphasizes deploying people into kingdom service, our team is made up of player-coaches. We have some superstars, but they're also great at coaching.

Building a team around our vision means that we would not hire a world-class performer who lacked the ability or passion to find, raise up, coach, and deploy others. No matter how gifted he might be, he wouldn't fit our vision. We'd pass on the opportunity.

Yet this same person might fit marvelously in a ministry that has another vision. For a church that's all about the weekend performance, the world-class performer would be a perfect fit. It all depends on the vision. People who struggle under one vision can flourish under another.

That's why successful and innovative leaders don't just find the best players. They find the best players who fit their vision. And depending on the specifics of the vision, some positions will be more important than others, and some traits essential in one setting won't be important in another.

It's the leader's job to know the difference. We can't just fill slots. We have to build a team, and we have to build it around the vision or else the vision will die.

4. *PRESERVE AND PROTECT* THE VISION AND VALUES

The final thing a leader can't delegate to others is the preservation and protection of the vision.

It's a leader's job to carefully consider how every change, innovation, opportunity, and program potentially impacts the vision. Few others will have the same global perspective that the leader has.

Everything we do has unintended consequences. A wise leader will think through these unintended consequences before giving the okay to something that might appear innocuous, because it's often the small things that undercut the vision — or send a powerful message about the vision.

For instance, the first time we outgrew our office space, we reshuffled the deck. We moved most of the staff to different buildings. But when I looked at the new office assignments, I noticed something that concerned me. Our small group pastor had been given a new office closer to his administrative team and farther from our top leaders.

On the surface that seemed like a great idea. Put the whole small group team together in one place to increase their teamwork and synergism.

But it wasn't a great idea. It was a bad idea.

It undercut our vision in a couple of ways.

Let me explain.

Our vision is to have small groups as the *hub* of our ministry. Yet this new office configuration put the head of our small group department in a different building from me, our executive pastor, and the other primary teaching pastor. It would have removed him from daily contact with our top leaders (out of sight is out of mind), and it would have sent a subtle message to the rest of the staff that his ministry was no more important than all the others, especially since he would no longer be down the hall from the top leaders.

I stepped in and made sure his office stayed near mine.

Now that might seem like a small thing. But it was a crucial step to preserving and protecting our vision. Years later things changed. Our top leaders were no longer concentrated in the same building. So the head of our small group ministry moved to be nearer to his team. A bad idea had become a good idea.

These are the type of things that only a leader with a thirty-thousand-foot global perspective can see. And these are the type of things that a leader needs to act upon. Successful serial innovators watch for unintended consequences. They pay attention to them. They don't make changes without making sure they support the vision.

• ◉ •

When it comes to vision, there are some things that only a leader can do. They can't be delegated. They can't be ignored. They have to be done. Successful serial innovators know and accept the fact that they not only have to ignite the vision; they also have to continually validate it, communicate it, build a team around it, and protect it.

Because if they don't. No one else will.

Part Seven

LEAVING A LEADERSHIP LEGACY

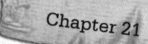

IT'S NOT ABOUT US

Leaving a Legacy of Change and Innovation

It's one thing to be a successful change agent or serial innovator.

It's still another thing to build a team that continues to morph and innovate over the long haul.

But rarer still are the leaders who leave behind a legacy of genuine openness to organizational change and innovation. These leaders not only innovate; they set the stage for future leaders to continue innovating long after they're gone.

I have experienced the joy of leading under the legacy of one who paved the way for future change and innovation. I've also known the frustration of trying to lead under the dark shadow of previous leaders whose policies and procedures tied my hands, making it nearly impossible to do what needed to be done.

That's why I'm so passionate about finding and empowering young eagles. It's also why I believe that paving the way for future leaders to fly as free and high as possible is one of the most important things a leader can do.

My greatest legacy will not be found in the changes and innovations that bear my name. It will be found in the corporate culture I leave behind. If I leave a legacy that encourages continual change and innovation, future leaders will rise up and call me blessed. If I

167

don't, they will call me something else. I can't put it in print. But you can guess.

To leave behind a legacy that supports and cultivates future change and innovation, three things will need to be in place *before* the next group of leaders takes the helm. Here's a brief look at each one.

1. THE FREEDOM TO ASK THE RIGHT QUESTIONS

To lead wisely, leaders need to continually ask and answer the following questions:

1. What is our unique mission?
2. What are our unique strengths and weaknesses?
3. What is current reality?
4. What do we need to do to better fulfill our mission?

But notice what they don't need to ask or know.

They don't need to know what their previous leaders would do if they were still in charge.

Trying to figure out what previous leaders would do is a waste of time. It's impossible to know. At best, we can know what they did in a different era, under different circumstances. But that doesn't tell us what they would do if they were in our shoes today. Even if the situations are exactly the same, the surrounding circumstances are not.

Yet the more innovative and successful our previous leaders were, the more likely it is that we'll look to them for guidance, not realizing that their ability to think outside the box in unpredictable ways is what made them great leaders.

What Would Walt Do?

It's reported that after Walt Disney's death, one of the most common questions asked among the new leadership team was, "What would Walt do?"

The result of asking that question was nearly two decades of slow decline. Even into the late 1970s, management was still asking what Walt would do, and then answering based on what he did in the 1950s and early '60s.

But had Walt still been alive, odds are he would have responded differently than he did back then. When he was alive, he was constantly adapting and seeing things from a fresh perspective. Certainly he would have continued to adapt and change in ways that no one can predict.

That's why Steve Jobs famously told Tim Cook right before his death to make sure no one at Apple asked, "What would Steve do?"[17]

Unfortunately, lots of leaders and leadership teams consider the "What would Walt do?" question to be a compliment. They're so sure that they've got it right that they can't imagine tomorrow's leaders needing to change anything. So they entrench today's policies, procedures, and programs deeply into the fabric of the organization. And in so doing, they make it nearly impossible for future leaders to innovate or lead.

Leaders Who Won't Trust

But there is something far worse than naively assuming that today's answers will solve all of tomorrow's questions. It's assuming that tomorrow's leaders can't be trusted.

Unfortunately, it's a mindset that is far more common than most people realize. It shows up when today's leaders lock down the options that future leaders will have in the fear that they might otherwise betray the mission. It's based on the assumption that people can't be trusted, especially the next generation. It's a toxic combination of arrogance and distrust that sabotages innovative leadership.

Most organizations have far too many rules and regulations. Many seem to be based on the belief that current staff and future leaders lack common sense.

For instance, consider the plethora of rules and regulations found within many churches, government agencies, unions, academia, and other bureaucratic organizations. While many of their guidelines and policies may be helpful, some are simply ridiculous. But far worse is something that no one seems to notice: the impact that having a rule for everything has on leaders. When everything is spelled out, there's no room for leadership. There's room only for enforcement.

It's no wonder low-trust organizations are seldom known for their cutting-edge or innovative policies and programs. They have to focus most of their energy on enforcing their rules rather than fulfilling their mission.

Another example can be found in the detailed constitutions and bylaws that control many ministries. I've seen some that spell out everything. Yes, I mean everything. They dictate the ratio of board members to constituents, lay out detailed job descriptions, specific staffing roles, salary structures, required programs, and even the schedule for worship services.

But ironically, these rigid rules designed to protect the mission always end up sabotaging the mission. They lock in policies and procedures that no longer work. They provide all the answers ahead of time, even when the questions have changed.

Expiration Dates

I've never met a leader who was grateful for a long list of rigid rules and regulations left behind by a previous leadership team. Most leaders are more than happy to listen to advice and learn from the past. But they hate to have their hands tied. And for good reason. To lead wisely, they must be free to ask and honestly answer, "What is the right thing to do in this situation, at this time?"

One of the best ways to provide future leaders with the freedom to continually ask that question is to make sure that all of our current policies, procedures, and programs have an expiration date — if not literally, figuratively.

Eventually, they'll all have to be tweaked or abandoned. So why not explicitly state that on the front end? And I mean explicitly. Whenever possible, let everyone know, "This is what we are doing for now; tomorrow may be different."

Ideally our policies and procedures let everyone know how we do things around here. They're simply statements and codifications of our best practices. And theoretically they should always be open to review and change.

But anyone who has led anything for ten minutes knows that organizational inertia quickly turns these policies and procedures into a sacred and eternal recipe. That's why I recommend that leaders constantly look for ways to remind everyone that the way we do things today may not be the way we do them tomorrow. If you beat that drum long enough and loudly enough, it will make it far easier on tomorrow's leaders when the expiration date finally comes.

2. THE FREEDOM TO DISAGREE

Tomorrow's leaders will also need the freedom to disagree with some of our fundamental and deeply held convictions—and the freedom to act on it.

Now, I'm not talking about moral issues. Right and wrong doesn't change over time.

But there are plenty of areas where we have deeply held leadership convictions that don't rise to the level of moral imperatives. I don't know what makes you pound the table. But I do know that every leader has a short list of nonnegotiables that aren't based on Scripture, morality, or integrity. They're simply reflections of our personal values and priorities.

One of the best things we can do to leave behind a legacy of continual change and innovation is to look for ways to make sure that those who follow us will have the freedom to do things we would never do. That means paving the way for them to lead in ways that are counter to our deeply held convictions about how things ought to be done.

For instance, when we sought the entitlements for our new main campus, one of the major impetuses behind our neighbors' fierce opposition was a clause in our use permit that allowed us to have a school on the premises (kindergarten through high school).

The irony is that I am not a fan of church schools. Possession is nine-tenths of the law. I find that those who use a classroom Monday through Friday eventually control what happens on the weekends.

Since I want North Coast to be a church for everyone, including those who don't have the funds to send their kids to a private school, I'm leery of anything that might undercut our ability to provide an incredible weekend experience for the kids who come. I want our classrooms to be themed with the Bible stories and the lessons we teach on the weekend, not pictures of past presidents and the alphabet.

Now you may disagree with me. That's not the issue. Time will tell. I could be wrong. But for today, one of my leadership nonnegotiables is that we will not have a K–12 school at North Coast as long as I'm in charge.

Yet none of our opponents knew this. So when they offered to settle the lawsuit if I would agree to drop the right to someday have a K–12 school, I burst out laughing. I felt like Brer Rabbit hearing that he'd been condemned to the briar patch.

Now this may surprise you. But our answer was no.

We refused to drop our right to have a school because, while it would have perfectly aligned with my leadership values and priorities, it also would have tied the hands of our future leaders. Codifying my nonnegotiables would have eliminated their right to disagree. So we continued with the lawsuit, losing both time and money, but ultimately gaining full flexibility and freedom for our future leaders.

Years down the road, if future leaders ever choose to revisit the church-school question, they'll be able to ask, "What does *God* want us to do?" It's a much better question than, "What did *Larry* want us to do?"

3. THE HUMILITY AND HONESTY TO HIGHLIGHT PAST FAILURES

The last thing that future leaders will need in order to freely innovate, make changes, and lead well is a humble and honest view of the past.

The problem is that our idealized memories of the past almost always look better than the harsh realities of the present. Given enough time, gory days turn into glory days, and pedestrian leaders begin to look like superstars.

If the past really did include glory days and initial leaders really were superstars, this can make it incredibly hard for the next set of leaders to lead.

That's why it's especially important for successful organizations and the leaders who help spearhead that success to be humble and honest enough to highlight and even memorialize their mistakes as well as their victories.

I think of a friend who followed a legendary leader. He did an admirable job. But every misstep was amplified under the microscope of an idealized image of his predecessor. Eventually, the comparisons became unbearable. So he stepped down.

Make no mistake, his predecessor was incredibly gifted and successful. But he was also far from perfect. He and his board made some goofy decisions that sabotaged the future. Long before he moved on, the massive crowds had already begun to wane, as well as his commitment and passion to the organization.

But that's not how anyone remembered it. Board members, lay leaders, and leftover staff romanticized the glory days and forgot all the pain that came with it. As a result, they fiercely resisted anything that seemed to break with the past, which made it impossible to halt their long and painful slide toward insignificance.

The only way to keep this from happening is to make sure that our failures are as well-known as our successes. That's one reason why I always talk about the "dark years" (my first three years at North Coast). I want people within our organization to know that I goofed up, made stupid decisions, and faced a season without growth. I also talk freely about the pain of an attempted coup, dumb financial decisions, and many other things that highlight my (and our current leadership team's) feet of clay.

No one wants to follow an idol, especially one that bears no resemblance to the real person.

· ● ·

Ultimately, all a leader can do is prepare the horse for battle. The outcome is out of our control. All we can do is make sure that we've done our best to create a climate of innovation and to foster an openness to change. We can light fires and pour gasoline on the ones who are already burning.

But at the end of the day, from a legacy standpoint, the most important thing we will ever do won't be found in the changes and innovations that bear our name. It will be found in the change agents and innovative leaders who stand on our shoulders.

ACKNOWLEDGMENTS

I want to express my gratitude to Ryan Pazdur and Andrew Rogers for believing in this project and shepherding it to completion. My best friend and wife, Nancy, and my assistant, Erica Brandt, provided honest feedback and initial editing that made a huge difference in the end product. Finally, to Paul Savona, Charlie Bradshaw, Chris Brown, Mike Yearley, and the North Coast board, thank you for trying lots of crazy ideas so that we could figure out the few that would change paradigms and take us and others toward our God-given goals.

NOTES

1. Between 1900 and 1920 there were almost two thousand firms involved in automobile production. Obviously, not many survived to tell their story (Paul Ormerod, *Why Most Things Fail: Evolution, Extinction, and Economics* [New York: Pantheon Books, 2005]; see also Wikipedia, "List of Automobile Manufacturers of the United States."

2. According to Marketdata Enterprise Inc., in a 2012 report titled "The U.S. Market for Self-Improvement Products and Services," as quoted by John LaRosa, Research Director, BS, MBA, Marketdata Enterprises, Inc., Tampa, FL, *http://www.prweb.com/releases/2012/3/prweb9323729.htm*.

3. The average firm lasts just fifteen years, and only 5 percent make it to year fifty (Claudio Feser, *Serial Innovators: Firms That Change the World* [Hoboken, NJ: Wiley, 2011], xiii). Up to one-fourth of all US commercial software projects were canned in 2000, costing firms a staggering 67 billion dollars (Robert Buderi, "Can Software Be Saved?" *Technology Review*, November 1, 2003, *http://www.technologyreview.com/news/402237/can-software-be-saved*, accessed May 2013).

4. Wikipedia, "Pet Rock," *http://en.wikipedia.org/wiki/Pet_Rock*, accessed October 2012.

5. See the works of Jim Collins and Peter Drucker for insights into the similarities and differences between leading a nonprofit and a for-profit organization. Particular insight can be found in Jim Collins, *Good to Great and the Social Sectors: A Monograph to Accompany "Good to Great"* (New York: HarperCollins, 2005), and Peter F. Drucker, *Managing the Non-Profit Organization: Principles and Practices* (New York: HarperCollins, 1992).

6. Joel Arthur Barker was the first to point out that the insights of Thomas Kuhn regarding scientific paradigms and discoveries also applied to the paradigm pioneers in the business world. His early videos and his book *Paradigms: The Business of Discovering the Future* (New York: HarperCollins, 1992) offers helpful insights into how social and organizational paradigms change, and into the people who change them.

7. Anthony Wing Kosner, "Jeff Bezos on How to Change Your Mind," *Forbes.com*, October 19, 2012, *http://www.forbes.com/sites/anthonykosner/2012/10/19/jeff-bezos-on-people-who-are-right-a-lot-vs-wrong-a-lot-has-he-got-it-right/*.

8. Peter Drucker, *Peter Drucker on the Profession of Management*, Harvard Business Review Books (Boston: Harvard Business School Publishing, 2003), 55.

9. "About Post-It Brand," Post-It Brand Products website, *http://www.post-it.com/wps/portal/3M/en_US/Post_It/Global/About/*.

10. Howard Schultz and Dori Jones Yang, *Pour Your Heart into It: How Starbucks Built a Company One Cup at a Time* (New York: Hyperion, 1999).

11. Peter Troxler, "Not Invented Here!" *Peter Troxler* (blog), June 2009, 7, *http://petertroxler.net/content/wp-content/uploads/2009/06/4.2-NotInventedHere.pdf*, accessed May 2013.

12. The story of Jethro advising Moses is found in Exodus 18.

13. Kevin B. O'Reilly, "Doctors Use Formula One Pit Crews as Safety Model," *American Medical News*, October 4, 2010, *http://www.amednews.com/article/20101004/profession/310049933/6/*, accessed April 2013.

14. For the entire passage, see 1 Corinthians 9:19–27.

15. The Winchester House was built by Sarah Winchester, the widow of gun magnate William Winchester. It was under constant construction from 1894 until Sarah's death in 1922. Many of the rooms make no sense. There are stairs to nowhere and many other oddities. After her death it became a tourist attraction, known for its purposeless construction.

16. Matthew 22:36–40.

17. Peter Burrows, "Apple's Jobs Told Cook Not To Ask 'What Would Steve Do?'" *Bloomberg*, October 25, 2011, *http://www.bloomberg.com/news/2011-10-25/apple-s-jobs-told-successor-cook-not-to-ask-what-would-steve-do-tech.html*, accessed April 2013.

About Leadership Network

Since 1984, Leadership Network has fostered church innovation and growth by diligently pursuing its far-reaching mission statement: *To identify high-capacity Christian leaders, to connect them with other leaders, and to help them multiply their impact.*

While specific techniques may vary as the church faces new opportunities and challenges, Leadership Network consistently focuses on bringing together entrepreneurial leaders who are pursuing similar ministry initiatives. The resulting peer-to-peer interaction, dialogue, and collaboration—often across denominational lines—helps these leaders better refine their individual strategies and accelerate their own innovations.

To further enhance this process, Leadership Network develops and distributes highly targeted ministry tools and resources, including books, DVDs and videotapes, special reports, e-publications, and free downloads.

For additional information on the mission or activities of Leadership Network, please contact:

Leadership ✖ Network

800-765-5323
www.leadnet.org
client.care@leadnet.org